On "Other War"

Lessons from Five Decades of RAND Counterinsurgency Research

Austin Long

Prepared for the
Office of the Secretary of Defense

Approved for public release;
distribution unlimited

NATIONAL DEFENSE
RESEARCH INSTITUTE

The research described in this report was prepared for the Office of the Secretary of Defense (OSD). The research was conducted in the the RAND National Defense Research Institute, a federally funded research and development center sponsored by the OSD, the Joint Staff, the Unified Combatant Commands, the Department of the Navy, the Marine Corps, the defense agencies, and the defense Intelligence Community under Contract W74V8H-06-C-0002.

Library of Congress Cataloging-in-Publication Data

Long, Austin.
    On "other war" : lessons from five decades of RAND counterinsurgency research / Austin Long.
        p. cm.
    "MG-482."
    Includes bibliographical references.
    ISBN 0-8330-3926-1 (pbk. : alk. paper)
    1. Counterinsurgency. I. Title.

U241.L66 2006
355.02'18—dc22

2006007106

The RAND Corporation is a nonprofit research organization providing objective analysis and effective solutions that address the challenges facing the public and private sectors around the world. RAND's publications do not necessarily reflect the opinions of its research clients and sponsors.

RAND® is a registered trademark.

Cover design by Stephen Bloodsworth
Cover photos: Left, *AP Photo/Abdel Kader Sahadi;* right, *AP Photo*

Published 2006 by the RAND Corporation
1776 Main Street, P.O. Box 2138, Santa Monica, CA 90407-2138
1200 South Hayes Street, Arlington, VA 22202-5050
4570 Fifth Avenue, Suite 600, Pittsburgh, PA 15213
RAND URL: http://www.rand.org/
To order RAND documents or to obtain additional information, contact
Distribution Services: Telephone: (310) 451-7002;
Fax: (310) 451-6915; Email: order@rand.org

Preface

The RAND Corporation's body of counterinsurgency (COIN) research, accumulated over the course of five decades, is an invaluable aid to understanding and developing successful responses to modern COIN challenges. This study seeks to summarize much of this research and make it readily accessible to a wider audience. It provides both the intellectual history of COIN theory and the elements of successful COIN campaigns.

This research was sponsored by the Office of the Secretary of Defense and conducted within the International Security and Defense Policy Center of the RAND National Defense Research Institute, a federally funded research and development center sponsored by the Office of the Secretary of Defense, the Joint Staff, the Unified Combatant Commands, the Department of the Navy, the Marine Corps, the defense agencies, and the defense Intelligence Community.

For more information on RAND's International Security and Defense Policy Center, contact the Director, James Dobbins. He can be reached by email at James_Dobbins@rand.org; by phone at 703-413-1100 x5134; or by mail at the RAND Corporation, 1200 South Hayes Street, Arlington, VA 22202-5050. More information about RAND is available at www.rand.org.

Contents

Figures

Summary

As part of the global war on terror, Operations Enduring Freedom and Iraqi Freedom showcased the dazzling technological capability and professional prowess of the U.S. military in conventional operations. Yet the subsequent challenges posed by insurgency and instability in both Afghanistan and Iraq have proved much more difficult to surmount for both the military and civilian agencies. Further, this difficulty in coping with insurgency may embolden future opponents to embrace insurgency as the only viable means of combating the United States. Thus, both the current and future conduct of the war on terror demand that the United States improve its ability to conduct counterinsurgency (COIN) operations. This study seeks to summarize much of what is known about prior COIN and to make recommendations for improving it based on the RAND Corporation's decades-long study of the subject.

The body of work generated from this study covers many aspects of COIN, from the most abstract theories of why insurgency takes place to tactical operations. It also covers a wide array of cases, varied in both geography and time, from the British experience in Malaya to the French in Algeria to the United States in El Salvador. However, the research is limited in that almost all of it is based on cases that occurred in the context of the Cold War. Some might question the continuing relevance of studies centered on conflicts that took place in such a radically different geopolitical context.

This study is based on the premise that, while many specific details do indeed vary greatly, insurgency and counterinsurgency is a more general phenomenon that is not a product of Cold War peculiarities. Further, many of the alleged differences between past and current COIN are overstated. For example, the fragmented nature of the insurgency in Iraq is often remarked on as almost without precedent. Yet many insurgencies during the Cold War were highly fragmented, with elements fighting each other as well as the counterinsurgent.

RAND was intimately involved in the formulation of the two major theories of how one should view the population, the battle space in COIN. The first theory, commonly called the "hearts and minds," or HAM, theory of COIN, argues that the impact of development and modernity on traditional societies causes the fragmentation of old institutions before new institutions are in place. This institutional gap creates problems, which can then give rise to insurgency. The prescription for success is therefore to win the public's support (their "hearts and minds") for the government by ameliorating some of the negative effects of development while speeding up the provision of modernity's benefits. RAND analysts felt that even if the actual provision of benefits lagged, the key was providing security to the population and convincing it that government was operating for its benefit.

Other researchers at RAND, steeped in economics and systems analysis, responded to this first theory by arguing that what mattered was not what the population thought but what it did. The key to the population was therefore to provide it with selective incentives to cooperate with the government and disincentives to resist the government.

In response to this "cost/benefit" theory, other RAND scholars pointed out that coercive methods could actually stimulate the insurgency, leading to spiraling escalation between insurgent and counterinsurgent, a spiral that might be unwinnable by modern democracies with moral and political limitations on the use of force.

In addition to more abstract theorizing, RAND researched elements of COIN practice. Four elements of particular relevance today are organization of insurgency and counterinsurgency, amnesty and reward programs, border control, and pacification. RAND conducted research on insurgent organization and sought to understand the strengths and weaknesses of these movements, particularly focusing on the Viet Cong in Vietnam. Through this research, RAND sought to understand more than the traditional military intelligence focus on the enemy order of battle, and included studies on insurgent learning and adaptation, motivation and morale, recruitment, and logistics. In addition, RAND worked to assess and develop new metrics for measuring progress against insurgent organizations, as traditional military indicators such as movement of the front or enemy killed were less relevant to COIN and might even be misleading.

RAND also conducted extensive research on the proper organization of government forces for COIN. The consensus of this research was the need for unity of effort between the political and military components of the government in order to ensure that the efforts of one did not undercut the progress of another. Further, RAND concluded that much of the U.S. military was overly focused on conventional war, leading to handicaps in the conduct of COIN.

The second element of COIN practice that RAND studied was the use of amnesty and reward programs to convince insurgents to surrender or to provide intelligence. In several cases, this approach proved both successful and cost-effective. In Malaya, an extensive reward program combined with informal amnesty for insurgents who cooperated against their former comrades worked very well. In Vietnam, the Chieu Hoi amnesty program was less successful than the Malayan experience, but it still led to the removal of thousands of insurgents from the Viet Cong at relatively low cost.

Border security was the third element studied by RAND, as many insurgencies rely on external support or cross-border sanctuaries. Sealing the borders could thus be very useful in COIN, as the French discovered in Algeria. The Morice Line sealed both the Tunisian and Moroccan borders to insurgents. RAND analysts, after initial skepticism about border security, began to advocate it in Vietnam as infiltration from the north became a bigger component of the war, though the system was never implemented.

The final category, pacification, is something of a catchall. It is best thought of as a combination of security and development in a given political unit (e.g., village or neighborhood). The central finding in RAND's pacification research was that it was by focusing on pacification in smaller political units, rather than ambitious plans for the nation as a whole, that progress could be made.

Several recommendations for current and future COIN can be derived from RAND's prior research. First, organization for COIN must be improved. The Provincial Reconstruction Team model that has been implemented in parts of Iraq and Afghanistan is a good start, but does not go far enough. This model, which unites U.S. civilian and military personnel with the local government, should be expanded and made the basis for current and future COIN efforts. Second, amnesty and reward programs should be implemented or expanded in COIN campaigns. These programs work in conjunction with military efforts to push insurgents out of the movement without having to fight them to literally the last person. A new study of insurgent motivation and morale should also be undertaken to provide greater insight into why insurgents fight. Third, given the cross-border elements of insurgency in both Iraq and Afghanistan, border security systems should be studied for both conflicts. Finally, pacification efforts should be focused on the lowest political echelons, and combined with census-taking and national identification cards.

Acknowledgments

Many people provided a great deal of help on this project. The author wishes to thank James Dobbins, William Rosenau, and Michael Lostumbo for their support of this project. Review comments provided by Bruce Hoffman of RAND and David Gompert of the National Defense University were insightful and challenging, for which the author is very grateful. Steve Hosmer was generous with his time in discussing RAND counterinsurgency research, much of which he participated in personally. Jeff Marquis was similarly generous with his historical expertise and provided extensive comments on the draft. The author's discussions about aspects of COIN with Bruce Nardulli and Jim Quinlivan were also very helpful. In addition to RAND colleagues, the author wishes to thank the members of the Massachusetts Institute of Technology (MIT) Center for International Studies Insurgency and Irregular Warfare Working Group for both formal and informal discussion, particularly Brendan Green, Colin Jackson, Jon Lindsay, Whitney Raas, Joshua Rovner, Paul Staniland, and Caitlin Talmadge. Also, conversations with both military and intelligence community personnel were invaluable in understanding current counterinsurgency efforts. Finally, the RAND library staff in both Washington and Santa Monica was very helpful with numerous requests for publications. The author extends special thanks to Leroy Reyes in Santa Monica and Gail Kouril in Washington for assistance with archival and classified material. Any errors remain the sole responsibility of the author.

Abbreviations

ACR	Armored Cavalry Regiment
APC	armored personnel carrier
ARPA	Advanced Research Projects Agency
ARVN	Army of the Republic of Vietnam
AUC	Autodefensas Unidas de Colombia (United Self-Defense of Colombia)
CAP	Combined Action Platoon
CIA	Central Intelligence Agency
CIDG	Civilian Irregular Defense Group
CIS	Center for International Studies
COIN	counterinsurgency
DEPCORDS	Deputy Commander for Civil Operations and Revolutionary Development Support
DVD	digital video disc
FFRDC	federally funded research and development center
FLN	Front de Liberation Nationale (National Liberation Front)
FMLN	Faribundo Marti para la Liberacion Nacional (Faribundo Marti Liberation Front)

GDP	gross domestic product
GVN	Government of Vietnam
HAM	hearts and minds
HES	Hamlet Evaluation System
IED	improvised explosive device
ISA	International Security Affairs
JASON	group of nongovernmental senior scientists established in 1960
KGB	Komitet gosudarstvennoi bezopasnosti (Committee for State Security)
MACV	Military Assistance Command Vietnam
MIT	Massachusetts Institute of Technology
MVD	Ministerstvo vnutrennykh del (Ministry of Internal Affairs)
NCO	noncommissioned officer
NLF	National Liberation Front
NSRD	National Security Research Division
NVA	North Vietnamese Army
OAS	Organisation de l'Armée Secrète (Secret Army Organization)
POW	prisoner of war
PRT	Provincial Reconstruction Team
RAND	Research and Development
RF/PF	Regional and Popular Forces
RIDA	Rural Industrial Development Authority

RPG	rocket-propelled grenade
RPV	remote-piloted vehicle
USAID	U.S. Agency for International Development
USCENTCOM	U.S. Central Command
USPACOM	U.S. Pacific Command
VC	Viet Cong
VM	Viet Minh

CHAPTER ONE

Introduction

It was an inextricable mess of things decent in themselves but that
human folly made look like the spoils of thieving.
        —*Joseph Conrad,* Heart of Darkness *(2004, p. 32)*

In a paper written in early 2004, Bruce Hoffman compared the U.S.
experience with counterinsurgency (COIN) to the movie *Groundhog
Day*, in which Bill Murray's character, Phil Connors, is forced to live
the same day over and over until he gets it right. Unlike Connors,
getting counterinsurgency right still appears to be a consummation
devoutly wished for the United States. In Iraq and Afghanistan, insurgents vex U.S. forces despite massive improvements in both technology
and training since the last deployment of combat troops for counterinsurgency in Vietnam.

This continued failure of the U.S. government to develop appropriate measures for counterinsurgency is all the more puzzling in light
of the effort devoted to understanding previous COIN campaigns.
Literally hundreds, if not thousands, of articles, monographs, and
books have been written on the topic by academics, analysts, military
officers, and journalists. Yet learning and adaptation by both civilian
and military organizations remain elusive.

The U.S. military in particular has had difficulty adapting to
COIN, in large part due to an overwhelming organizational focus on
conflict with peer competitors and conventional warfare contingency

operations.[1] The term "other war," meaning pacification operations, arose in Vietnam to differentiate those operations from the "real war" of conventional search-and-destroy operations. This focus on high-intensity conflict has, perhaps ironically, resulted in such overwhelming superiority in nuclear and conventional military capability that opponents (with a few possible exceptions) are forced to embrace low-intensity conflict as the only viable means of challenging the United States.[2] In Iraq and Afghanistan, rapid and overwhelming conventional success has been countered by terrorism and insurgency. Adaptation and learning about COIN have thus become critical for the military in the 21st century.

For almost five decades, RAND has been at the forefront of the effort to improve learning on COIN, conducting extensive research beginning in the late 1950s. This book is an attempt to examine much of this work in light of current COIN, in hopes of reducing the amount of "reinventing of the wheel" that is necessary for the United States to improve its capabilities for COIN both in the present and future. It is thus part intellectual history and part policy recommendation, with the goal of encouraging the type of serious introspection by the U.S. government that will be needed to get COIN right. The lessons of the past, with due consideration for changes in the global security environment, should be applied in Iraq, Afghanistan, and wherever else the United States may need to wage low-intensity conflict.

The book consists of five substantive chapters. The first presents a brief history of COIN research at RAND to provide context for the reader. Next is a short discussion of the benefits and perils of using previous experience as a guide to current COIN. The third section is an overview of the development of COIN theories at RAND and some suggestions for synthesizing those theories. The fourth examines RAND's analysis of the practice of COIN in a number of conflicts in an attempt to draw out "best practices" for today. The last chapter is an

---

[1]   This focus is not universal in the military. For example, the U.S. Army Special Forces have traditionally excelled in unconventional warfare. However, the conventional focus dominates most of the broader military.

[2]   See Posen (2003) for a discussion of U.S. conventional advantage and its limitations.

admittedly tentative attempt to apply these practices to the present. In addition, an annotated bibliography of much of the RAND research on which this book is based is provided as an appendix. Some of the documents cited herein were part of RAND's D series of publications, which were intended to promote discussion among researchers. Those publications were not reviewed and were never intended for external dissemination, yet provide interesting insights into the debate with RAND on these issues at the time. Not all D-series publications are available to the public.

CHAPTER TWO

The Wizards of Less-Than-Armageddon: RAND and COIN

As World War II drew to a close, the Commanding General of the Army Air Forces was concerned about the future. Airpower and technology appeared inextricably tied together, particularly in the dawning atomic age. Yet General Henry "Hap" Arnold was worried that, without the impetus of war, U.S. scientists would return to universities, depriving the military of their expertise. In order to ensure access to elite intellectual talent, Arnold and others in and out of government established the Research and Development (RAND) Corporation in October 1945. RAND quickly grew into an interdisciplinary think tank concerned with the problems of the nascent Cold War (see Digby, 1991; Martin Collins, 1998; and Andrew May, 1999).

In these early years, RAND's primary focus was on the problems of the Air Force, particularly the nuclear forces of the Strategic Air Command. Analysts such as Albert and Roberta Wohlstetter, Herman Kahn, Andrew Marshall, William Kaufmann, and Thomas Schelling grappled with a variety of questions for the Air Force, ranging from the strategic to the tactical (see Kaplan, 1991). Optimal basing strategies for bombers, game theoretic approaches to escalation and deterrence, and avoiding surprise attack were some of the central questions they sought to address.

Counterinsurgency had not entered the lexicon of defense planners at RAND in this period. The first attempt to address the problem came in 1958, with a set of war games at RAND known as Sierra (Paxson, 1958). These war games sought to explore the possibility of limited war in Asia in light of the U.S. experience in Korea and the

French war in Indochina. Sierra envisioned the fighting as semiconventional, mirroring the later stages of the French conflict in Indochina. Large enemy formations and the possible use of atomic weapons were considered and evaluated in several scenarios.

This work was consonant with the feeling among many at RAND and in the government that reliance on strategic nuclear forces for deterrence was uncertain.[1] The threat to resort to launching so-called "Massive Retaliation" was not credible below a certain threshold, particularly in conflicts outside the United States or Western Europe (see Gaddis, 1982). Former Army Chief of Staff General Maxwell Taylor was perhaps the most vocal and widely recognized critic of what he saw as overreliance on strategic nuclear forces. In his 1960 book *The Uncertain Trumpet*, Taylor advocated a policy calling for a buildup of conventional and tactical nuclear forces to allow for a more flexible response to provocation below the threshold for total war.

The inauguration of John F. Kennedy in 1961 marked a major turning point in U.S. strategy, particularly in response to the problem of Third World insurgency. Kennedy adopted Taylor's slogan of "Flexible Response" as his own, but expanded it to cover insurgencies as well as limited wars such as those envisioned by Sierra. Kennedy was also keenly interested in attracting the "best and brightest" minds to his administration, and several RAND personnel came to Washington as a result. This both deepened and broadened RAND's ties to the government, as it could increasingly work on problems not directly tied to and funded by the Air Force.[2]

As the Kennedy administration took office, an insurgency was gaining strength in South Vietnam, one of the countries formed by the dissolution of French Indochina following the French loss to insurgents in 1954. The United States had committed itself to supporting an independent, non-communist South Vietnam, but the government of

---

[1]   Albert Wohlstetter was one among many at RAND concerned with this problem of U.S. strategy. See Wohlstetter (1958).

[2]   See Wells (2001) and Ghamari-Tabrizi (2005) for insight into RAND at the time. Among notable RAND analysts who took jobs in the administration were Charles Hitch, Alain Enthoven, and Henry Rowen.

Ngo Dien Diem was increasingly unable to resist insurgents supported by communist North Vietnam. U.S. advisors were aiding the South Vietnamese; military assistance was flowing quite freely but seemed to do little to stanch the erosion of the government's authority.[3]

RAND would quickly become intimately involved with both the general problem of counterinsurgency and the specific problem of Vietnam. Analysts such as Guy Pauker, George Tanham, and Stephen Hosmer (among many others; Figure 2.1 shows the latter) began intensive investigation of previous counterinsurgency campaigns in an attempt to derive lessons. RAND brought in participants in these campaigns as consultants and held several symposia seeking patterns in insurgency and counterinsurgency.[4] The Assistant Secretary of Defense for International Security Affairs (ISA) and the Advanced Research Projects Agency (ARPA) funded most of this research.

Over the next several years, U.S. involvement in South Vietnam continued to escalate incrementally. RAND's research expanded in parallel, leading to the establishment of a permanent presence in a French colonial villa in Saigon. From this location, RAND researchers traveled the country, gathering and assessing data. RAND's Santa Monica office also had an entire room dedicated to Vietnam, which included RAND products, captured Viet Cong documents, and U.S. intelligence reports.

During this period, one of the largest RAND projects on counterinsurgency, the Viet Cong Motivation and Morale Study, was initiated. With funding from ISA and ARPA, RAND was tasked to discover what motivated the Viet Cong and how they could be influenced. This entailed conducting and analyzing hundreds of interviews with captured and surrendered Viet Cong and their supporters.[5]

---

[3]   For an overview of U.S. attempts to build South Vietnamese internal security, see Rosenau (2005).

[4]   One of the best of these symposia, chaired by Stephen Hosmer, took place in April 1962. The participants included such well-known COIN practitioners as David Galula, Anthony Jeapes, Frank Kitson, and Edward Landsdale. See Hosmer and Crane (1963).

[5]   For an overview of the Motivation and Morale Study, see Davison (1972).

Figure 2.1
RAND Analyst Stephen Hosmer

SOURCE: RAND archives.
RAND MG482-2.1

RAND analysts would contest the findings of the Motivation and Morale study, a symptom of increasing divergence within RAND on Vietnam. Leon Gouré was representative of one school of thought, optimistic about the findings and the war generally, believing the Viet Cong to be increasingly hard-pressed and dispirited (see, among others, Gouré and Thomson, 1965). Konrad Kellen represented the opposite school of thought, increasingly questioning the viability of U.S. involvement in Vietnam and finding the Viet Cong well-motivated and disciplined in the face of incredible hardship (see, among others, Kellen, 1969b).

This division between those at RAND (like Gouré) who were more sanguine about the prospects for U.S. success in Vietnam and those who felt the effort unlikely to succeed (like Kellen) mirrored the emerging split in the country between "hawks" and "doves." This split emerged publicly in October 1969, when a group of RAND researchers sent a letter to the editor of *The New York Times* calling for U.S. withdrawal from Vietnam. Subsequently, another group of RAND analysts sent a rejoinder to *The Times* countering the first letter's arguments (see Roberts, 1969a, 1969b).

Despite the emerging fissures within RAND, research on counterinsurgency continued to expand for the duration of U.S. involvement in Vietnam. ARPA created a special research program, Project AGILE, dedicated to analyzing the problems of counterinsurgency in Southeast Asia. AGILE funded many additional RAND studies, ranging from assessing measures of effectiveness in counterinsurgency to understanding the rural population (for example, Benoit, 1970; and Sweetland, 1968).

The Vietnam conflict (more specifically, U.S. involvement in the conflict) finally began to wind down in the early 1970s, and with it U.S. government interest in counterinsurgency. As the interest of sponsors went, so went RAND research. RAND produced a few more "lessons learned" products from participants in the Vietnam conflict, but by 1972, RAND was all but out of the counterinsurgency business as interest returned to the conventional defense of Western Europe and strategic nuclear forces.[6] The unhealed divisions within RAND over Vietnam and the unauthorized release of the classified "Pentagon Papers" by Daniel Ellsberg, which had significant negative repercussions for RAND, no doubt added to the desire of many to put counterinsurgency behind them.[7]

This fallow period would last nearly a decade, as both the Ford and Carter administrations had little appetite for anything remotely related to Vietnam or counterinsurgency. RAND was fortunate to retain many researchers with counterinsurgency experience, but they were tasked with other questions. For example, RAND analyst and

---

[6] These included Komer (1972a) and Koch (1973). The last major RAND study on Vietnam, including COIN, was commissioned just after the fall of Saigon in 1975 (see Hosmer, Kellen, and Jenkins, 1978).

[7] See Wells (2001, pp. 416–419 and 453–457) for commentary on how the Pentagon Papers affected RAND.

former director of civilian programs in Vietnam Bob Komer went to work on issues of coalition warfare and NATO policy (for example, see Komer et al., 1973).

One refuge for counterinsurgency specialists at RAND was the growing concern among the policy community over the issue of international terrorism. The late 1960s and early 1970s saw an explosion of terrorist activity, from the Munich massacre by the Palestinian Black September organization to various "Red" terrorist groups in Europe to the Weather Underground in the United States. Researchers such as Konrad Kellen and Brian Jenkins quickly transitioned to the intensive study of terrorist motivation, strategy, and tactics (for example, see Kellen, 1979; and Jenkins, 1974).

The doldrums of RAND COIN research ended in the early 1980s, as the Reagan administration became increasingly concerned about insurgency in Latin America, particularly Central America. The fall of the Somoza regime in Nicaragua to the communist Sandinistas and an ongoing insurgency in El Salvador rekindled fears of a Central American "domino effect" that ultimately could threaten the stability of the hemisphere. This threat to the "Southern Flank" enabled RAND to pursue research again on COIN, though not at the same volume and intensity experienced during the Vietnam era.

In this period, new analysts such as Bruce Hoffman and Benjamin Schwarz joined old hands from Vietnam.[8] In addition to examining the Salvadoran conflict itself, RAND analysts assessed post-Vietnam COIN efforts in an attempt to draw lessons for current and future

---

[8] For example, see Hosmer and Tanham (1986); Hoffman, Taw, and Arnold (1991); and Schwarz (1991). The latter two publications reflect the fact that RAND was still not unified in views of COIN. Published the same year but for different sponsors, the two were quite different in tone. The Hoffman, Taw, and Arnold report, while noting the difficulties of COIN, sought to make recommendations to improve COIN in El Salvador. The Schwarz report was quite pessimistic in tone and questioned continued U.S. involvement in El Salvador. As in the split over Vietnam-era COIN, the two differed less on the facts themselves than on the appropriate response. Hoffman, Taw, and Arnold saw little alternative to improving COIN in El Salvador given the stakes, while Schwarz felt that the cause was all but beyond saving. This author thanks Bruce Hoffman, project leader of the studies that produced both reports, for clarifying this debate.

conflicts. The transitioning of the Arroyo Center, the Army's federally funded research and development center (FFRDC), to RAND in 1984 also presented new funding opportunities for COIN research.

However, just as RAND COIN research began to regain momentum, the Cold War ended. This dramatically reduced interest in COIN within the policy community, and many of the Central American insurgencies came to an end. Without this impetus, RAND COIN research slowed again. However, unlike the post-Vietnam period, it did not come to a halt. RAND researchers continued to investigate COIN subjects, such as the trend in urbanization of insurgency and developing strategic frameworks for COIN (see Taw and Hoffman, 1994; and Hoffman and Taw, 1992). In addition, RAND increasingly linked COIN to other topics of interest to policymakers, such as terrorism or stability operations (for example, Meyer, Duncan, and Hoffman, 1993; and Quinlivan, 1995). RAND research on COIN thus analyzed and drew lessons widely from across both space (from Malaya to El Salvador) and time (from the late 1940s through the 1990s).[9]

---

[9] See, for example, the recent cross-national RAND survey in Byman et al. (2001).

CHAPTER THREE

Analogies and War: Are Theory and Empirics from Prior COIN Relevant?

Before proceeding, it is worth discussing the merit of studying previous COIN theory and practice. Some consider valueless any attempts to develop a generalizable theory of COIN or to seek analogies to other conflicts, as each insurgency is deeply rooted in a particular set of conditions, both domestic and international. Only an analyst with great depth in a given region or country can make judgments about it, obviating the need for theory or analogy.

Answering these objections involves an issue that is at the core of both social science and policy analysis, and this particular work more so than many others. This issue is that of analogical reasoning, or more simply, what can previous problems tell us about (or mislead us in) thinking through a new problem? From this issue of analogical reasoning springs the question of generalizability, or what can a few specific examples of some type tell us about all examples of this type?[1] More specifically, what theories and practices appear to work generally in COIN and how can they be applied today?

Although these questions are relevant in all types of scientific inquiry, they are perhaps paramount in social science and policy analysis. In both disciplines, a "nasty, untidy mess" often confronts the

---

[1] There is a considerable body of work on historical analogy and foreign policy. See, for example, Khong (1992), Ernest May (1973), and Neustadt and May (1986).

researcher.[2] Unlike the physical sciences, controlled experiments are quite hard to come by, and many problems have a great many variables present, often interacting in unobservable ways. History in many cases becomes the ersatz laboratory for both disciplines.

The problem then becomes one of choosing appropriate analogies, acknowledging the inevitable differences between past and present, and then attempting to arrive at generalizable conclusions. It may seem laborious to discuss this process, which is probably ingrained in most social scientists and policy analysts by training and experience. Yet in the current political climate, analogies about COIN are being accepted, rejected, and contested at a furious pace in academia, policy circles, and op-ed pages.[3]

This discussion is also one with historical precedent, having occurred at RAND during and after Vietnam. In the best tradition of RAND, researchers brought an open-minded but skeptical approach to COIN and were often quick to acknowledge the limits of research methods and conclusions. Some at RAND during this period felt that, given the tentative state of research results on Vietnam, attempting to draw lessons from it for the future was perilous. Wohlstetter (1968a, p. 1) famously wrote, "Of all the disasters of Vietnam, the worst may be the 'lessons' that we'll draw from it." Similarly, Melvin Gurtov and Konrad Kellen authored a paper in 1969 titled *Vietnam: Lessons and Mislessons.*

Yet none of these authors rejected the drawing of lessons for the future. Instead, they counseled caution and reflection in doing so. In a short appendix to *On Vietnam and Bureaucracy*, Wohlstetter (1968a) provides his own observations on what happened in Vietnam as a start-

---

[2] This quotation is particularly apt and is taken from Theodore Sorenson's account of President Kennedy's view of U.S. involvement in South Vietnam (Sorensen, 1965, pp. 660–661).

[3] Even a casual search of the *Early Bird*, the Department of Defense's clipping service, for the month of August 2005 finds more than a dozen articles that propose or reject analogies between Iraq and Vietnam. For example, see Jacoby (2005) and Gerwehr and Hachigian (2005). Politicians ranging from Republican Senator Chuck Hagel to Democratic Senator Ted Kennedy have also made reference to Vietnam analogies with respect to Iraq. Andrew Krepinevich (2005) draws extensively on the Vietnam analogy in *How to Win in Iraq*.

ing point for lessons. He further noted, "Lessons from such complex events require much reflection to be of more than negative worth. But reactions to Vietnam . . . tend to be visceral rather than reflective" (p. 1).

It is with this attitude of reflection that the theoretical and empirical challenges of "the lessons of history" should be approached. The question asked should not be whether Iraq and Afghanistan are new Vietnams. Instead, with an open but skeptical mind, two related questions should be posed. First, how much is any specific insurgency (and counterinsurgency) an example of a general phenomenon? Second, how are specific (as opposed to general) characteristics similar or different when comparing two insurgencies?

A definitive answer to those two questions is beyond the scope of the present work (and may be impossible at present, given the number of unknowns in Iraq and Afghanistan). However, this study is premised on the assertion that Iraq and Afghanistan are consonant with some general characteristics of insurgency and counterinsurgency, and are more similar to than different from many previous insurgencies. There is some prima facie evidence to support this point, though it is far from definitive.[4]

The general characteristics of insurgency are easily recognized in Iraq and Afghanistan. Senior officials in the military and government, after some initial reluctance, have embraced the term *insurgency* in classifying the conflicts in both Iraq and Afghanistan. The first "strategic pillar" of the *National Strategy for Victory in Iraq* is "Defeat the Terrorists and Neutralize the Insurgency" (NSC, 2005, p. 28).

The central characteristic of insurgency is the reliance on population for active support or at least passive acquiescence. This support, whether from affinity with or coercion from the insurgents (often a mix of both) provides the insurgents with personnel, supplies, and, critically, an information advantage over the counterinsurgent force. While theories (discussed in detail in the next chapter) have been developed to model this link between the insurgent and the population, all agree on

---

[4]   See Beckett (2005), Sepp (2005), and Lynn (2005) for three recent works that accept this premise.

its importance. In both Iraq and Afghanistan, it is this link that allows insurgents to attack coalition forces or to plant improvised explosive devices (IEDs), and then fade back into the population.

If the general characteristics of insurgency are present in Iraq and Afghanistan, what about specific differences between these present COIN efforts and past campaigns? Some argue that the end of the Cold War and the rise of militant Islam, among other factors, have made COIN in the 21st century qualitatively different from that of the 20th century. For example, one of the most remarked upon aspects of the Iraqi insurgency is that it appears to be a "coalition of the willing" that opposes the United States, the current Iraqi government, and their allies rather than a unified movement with common goals. Jihadists, Ba'athists, criminals, and various tribes all appear to be major components of the insurgency, which lacks any central command structure or ideology. Some allege this to be a new and surprising phenomenon, unlike previous insurgencies (for example, see Bennet, 2005).

Yet examination of many previous insurgencies finds that many began in this fashion, and several successful insurgencies never developed either a common ideology or an effective central command. El Salvador's Faribundo Marti para Liberacion Nacional (FMLN) was a fairly loose coalition of "five and a half" factions that only developed a rudimentary central command structure at the behest of its external supporters in Cuba and the Soviet Union.[5] The same is true of the mujahideen who fought the Soviets in Afghanistan, who ranged in character from the proto–al Qaeda jihadists of Osama bin Laden to the relatively secular Tajik force of Ahmad Shah Masood to the opportunistic Pashtun Gulbuddin Hekmatyar's Hezb-e Islami. They had essentially no central command either, other than pressures to cooperate imposed by their external sponsors in the United States, Pakistan, and Saudi Arabia. These factions almost immediately fell to fighting one another after the final collapse of the communist regime (see Coll, 2004).

Even the Viet Cong, supposedly a model of organizational cohesion, was less unified initially than is often noted. The National

---

[5]   For discussion of the fragmentary nature of the FMLN, see CIA (1984).

Liberation Front (NLF), which was the Vietnamese equivalent of the FMLN, was dominated by communists but included a variety of nationalist elements.[6] Technique and ideology in the early part of the insurgency varied both by region and by individual. These differences, while lessening greatly as the war progressed, were never entirely resolved. The communists turned on their allies as soon as the war was over, in some cases sending them to "reeducation camps" alongside many former South Vietnamese government officials.[7]

Further, much of the pressure from the government's security apparatus that forces insurgents to become better organized is lacking in Iraq and Afghanistan. In both countries, many of the most basic elements of this apparatus are not merely ineffective: They are nonexistent. This is in marked contrast to previous counterinsurgencies, such as Vietnam, where the security apparatus might have been both corrupt and somewhat inept, but was still a force in being. In fact, this lack of government institutions in much of Iraq and Afghanistan reduces the need for insurgents to develop so-called "counterinstitutions," as there is often nothing to "counter."

This is not to argue that nothing about the Iraqi insurgency is new or different. The use of the Internet and DVD as propaganda and communication tools is certainly new (though not unprecedented, as the Mexican Chiapas rebels in the 1990s made use of the Internet) (see Coll and Glasser, 2005). The fact that the countryside is practically awash in ordnance ranging from assault rifles and rocket-propelled

---

[6] The degree to which the NLF was an appendage of the Communist Party remains contested. Stephen Hosmer (1970, esp. pp. 6–8), arguing that the NLF was a convenient fiction, notes the pervasive influence of the North Vietnamese communist security apparatus in the South. However, both Douglas Pike (1966, Chapter Four, esp. p. 82) and William Duiker (1996, Chapter Eight, esp. pp. 210–213) note that while the NLF was certainly formed and dominated by the North, it was not entirely a convenient, fictional organization either, having some independence and genuine noncommunist participation. The point here is that even the best example of a "monolithic" insurgency was not as cohesive as is often believed.

[7] See Tang, Chanoff, and Doan (1985). Tang was a senior NLF official, whose views also support the nonmonolithic nature of the insurgency in the South.

grenades (RPGs) to artillery shells and bombs is substantially different from almost all previous insurgencies, which often needed external support for weapons.[8]

More broadly, Iraq and Afghanistan are, despite some convergence in tactics of the insurgents, only loosely linked by elements of transnational jihad. Much of the insurgency in both countries (though certainly not all) is linked to specific local grievances based on ethnicity. In Iraq, Sunni Arabs who feel that they have lost their primacy are the main supporters of the insurgency. Foreign fighters appear to make up a dangerous but small minority of combatants.[9] In Afghanistan, aggrieved ethnic Pashtuns who straddle the Pakistani border appear to be paramount in supporting the insurgency. In contrast, the challenge in Vietnam, El Salvador, and many other Cold War insurgencies was manifestly linked to Communist support of "wars of national liberation," even if the insurgency was deeply rooted in local conditions and grievances.

However, these differences should not obscure the fundamental similarities between past and present insurgencies. Insurgency is a method of war, in the same way that combined-arms blitzkrieg is one. The context of the method and some elements of the method may change, but the fundamentals do not. The massive armored single envelopment conducted by the U.S. VII Corps in 1991 would have been readily recognizable to a German general in 1941 or to an Israeli general in 1967, despite differences in context. Indeed, U.S. Central Command (USCENTCOM) Commander Gen. Norman Schwarzkopf is alleged to have examined German tank operations during World War II while planning for Desert Storm. Similarly, despite differences in context and some elements, past insurgencies offer valuable insight into combating present ones.

---

[8]   See Richey (2003). The volume of munitions available globally, even apart from Iraq, is also high in the post–Cold War period as the Warsaw Pact countries liquidate their arsenals.

[9]   See Finer (2005). Estimates of foreign fighter numbers range from 4 percent to 10 percent of the total number of insurgents.

Note, too, that overall success in war, whether conventional or COIN, depends on a variety of factors and the overall success or failure of a military effort should be used carefully to judge the utility of specific elements of that effort. For example, the Wehrmacht that Gen. Schwarzkopf studied in 1991 was decisively defeated in 1945, yet remains admired for its operational and tactical excellence. Similarly, one should not ignore previous efforts simply because they ultimately failed, as the U.S. military ignored French efforts in Indochina as it went into Vietnam.[10] "Lessons learned" should be evaluated for their positive and negative contributions to the overall COIN effort.

Finally, some would argue that the current challenge of al Qaeda, conceived of as a global insurgency with goals transcending individual nation-states, presents a radically different problem than previous COIN efforts have faced. This conception and resulting dismissal of prior COIN is problematic. First, it is not clear that conceiving of al Qaeda as a global insurgency provides valuable analytic insight. For example, the September 11 attacks were not part of an attempt by al Qaeda to take over the United States. Rather, it was, among other things, an attempt to force changes in U.S. foreign policy that would make revolution and insurgency easier in certain parts of the Muslim world, most notably Saudi Arabia.

Second, even if al Qaeda is best thought of as an insurgency, it is all the more imperative that the methods used to defeat previous insurgencies, most, if not all, of which enjoyed external support, be applied. If anything, it calls for successful COIN practice to be applied outside of those nations where U.S. forces are directly engaged in combat but that are sources of significant support for the transnational jihad that al Qaeda supposedly represents. The most obvious starting points would be Egypt and Saudi Arabia, two of the largest and wealthiest Arab countries and major sources of jihadists. The key point is that, regardless of whether the goals of insurgency end at the nation-state level or transcend it, the nation-state is the battleground for insurgents. If nation-states can defeat insurgents within their borders, then sporadic and localized terrorism will be the best for which the would-be trans-

---

[10] For comments on this ignorance, see Starry (1979, pp. 4–6) and Record (1998, p. 47).

national insurgents can hope. After all, despite its protean nature and ability to reconstitute itself, al Qaeda's global reach was undoubtedly badly damaged by the defeat of its Taliban allies in Afghanistan.

A separate, but perhaps even more relevant, source of resistance to COIN theorizing is that, after Vietnam, it is not something in which either the policy or academic communities wish to be involved. The divisions at RAND over Vietnam mentioned previously were mild compared to the divisions in those communities, and many simply avoided the subject as much as possible. The slogan "No more Vietnams" was popular not only with peace activists, but many in government and the professional military (essentially this was the basis of the Weinberger-Powell Doctrine).[11] While this attitude is understandable, it is simply no longer tenable in the 21st century, when the United States is faced with the prospect of few if any major conventional wars but potentially many insurgencies.

---

[11] The Weinberger-Powell Doctrine argued that the U.S. military should only be committed with clear objectives, overwhelming force, and in situations that were vital to U.S. security. First articulated by Secretary of Defense Caspar Weinberger at a National Press Club meeting in 1984, it was developed in consultation with his military assistant, future Chairman of the Joint Chiefs Colin Powell.

CHAPTER FOUR
COIN Theory: What Are Insurgencies and How Does One Fight Them?

COIN theory (as opposed to lists of practices such as those codified in works such as the U.S. Marine Corps *Small Wars Manual* [1972]) is almost entirely a product of the Cold War. It resulted from the interaction of government and academia that was so common in the decades between the beginning of World War II and the end of Vietnam. RAND was one of the premier entities for facilitating this interaction, and so is central to the development of COIN theory. The next chapter traces the evolution of two competing theories of COIN, and then makes suggestions for further development of theory.

"Hearts and Minds" Theory: COIN as a Problem of Modernization

The development of COIN theory began in the early 1950s among academics, most notably at the Central Intelligence Agency (CIA)–sponsored Center for International Studies (CIS) at the Massachusetts Institute of Technology.[1] Many of the scholars at CIS were well known to RAND researchers, and ideas were shared between them. For example, CIS and RAND both worked to develop war-gaming and crisis-

---

[1] For detail on the intellectual history of COIN theory, see Shafer (1988) and Marquis (2000). For a history of CIS and its COIN research, see Blackmer (2002).

simulation techniques in the 1950s and 1960s.[2] Lucian Pye in particular worked as a consultant to RAND from the early 1960s on. CIS faculty joining RAND researchers during the Kennedy administration further cemented these ties.[3]

The initial focus of COIN research was on the problems of modernization and economic development. Scholars observed that, in many societies, the negative consequences of economic development to which the developed nations adjusted over the course of decades and centuries were being experienced in the space of years by the developing countries. As the economic conditions underlying society began to shift, pressure built on traditional society. This, in turn, put pressure on nascent governments, many of which had only recently acquired independence from colonial empires, and on those empires that sought to retain their colonies. In many cases, governmental institutions could not keep pace with societal change, leading to disorder and instability. This instability also left societies vulnerable to external Communist influence.[4]

Insurgents could thus take advantage of this flux to gain popular support, by promising alternatives to the government. The government, unable to ameliorate the problems of the population, would increasingly be isolated and weakened. The insurgents could acquire almost everything they needed from the populace, progressively attenuating government authority and creating "counterinstitutions" to provide what the government could or would not (e.g., taxation or social services). Eventually, either the government would collapse, unable to separate the insurgents from the people, or the insurgents could form their own armies and defeat the government in battle. This was the

---

[2]   See Thomas B. Allen (1987). Herbert Goldhamer of RAND and Lincoln Bloomfield of CIS are credited as two of the major developers of political-military exercises.

[3]   Most notably, Walt Rostow was Kennedy's first Deputy National Security Adviser and then Chair of the Policy Planning Committee at the State Department.

[4]   See Rostow (1959) and Pye (1958) for early thoughts on these issues. Samuel Huntington's *Political Order in Changing Societies* (1968) remains the definitive work on the tension between political development and order.

essence of what Mao called "people's war," and many Western scholars adopted the Maoist viewpoint on insurgency (see, for example, Mao, 1961; and Giap, 1963).

Once these two principles, the problems of modernization and the insurgent need for popular support, were accepted, the solution became apparent. The answer was to restore the hope of the people and gain their support for the government. In order to do this, COIN would consist of providing the people security from predations by government and insurgent forces and reducing the negative consequences of development while enhancing the positive aspects. Increasing political rights of the people, improving standards of living, and reducing corruption and abuse of government power were key prescriptions of this COIN theory, which came to be known as "winning the hearts and minds of the people," a term coined by Sir Gerald Templer during the Malayan Emergency.

Shortened to "hearts and minds" (HAM) theory, this theory was accepted, if not uncritically, by many at RAND. Riley Sunderland (1964c) devoted an entire volume of his five-volume treatise on British COIN in Malaya to the subject. Guy Pauker doubted the actual extent of improvement in living standards experienced by the people in successful COIN efforts, but argued for the importance of "reawakening the people's confidence and hope through convincing evidence that the government did care about their welfare" (1962, p. 12). In discussing the generally effective COIN doctrine of the Indonesian military, Pauker noted, "The concept of 'winning the hearts and minds of the people' . . . was a guiding principle of the Indonesian military, although they did not use those tainted words" (Pauker, 1985, p. 21).

HAM theory was the dominant paradigm for COIN in the early 1960s. Both practitioners and theoreticians alike considered popular support the sine qua non of COIN.[5] However, some RAND researchers began to question this paradigm as U.S. involvement in Vietnam increased.

---

[5] For an example of a practitioner's views, see Melnik (1964, pp. 76–86).

Cost/Benefit Theory: Carrots and Sticks for the Rational Peasant

In 1965, as the United States crossed the Rubicon of deploying ground forces to Vietnam, RAND economist Charles Wolf, Jr. (shown in Figure 4.1), circulated a paper questioning the validity of one of the central precepts of HAM theory. Wolf argued that popular support was far from necessary for insurgents in lesser-developed countries. He pointed out: "From an operational point of view, what an insurgent movement requires for successful and expanding operations is not popular support, in the sense of attitudes of identification and allegiance, but rather a supply of certain inputs . . . at a reasonable cost, interpreting cost to include expenditure of coercion as well as money" (1965, p. 5).

Figure 4.1
RAND Economist Charles Wolf, Jr.

SOURCE: RAND archives.
RAND *MG482-4.1*

Wolf further attacked the argument that increasing the standard of living through development would reduce insurgency. In effect, development made more resources available to citizens, which insurgents could then acquire from the population through persuasion, coercion, or a combination of the two. Thus, paradoxically, programs designed to reduce popular support for insurgents could actually reduce the insurgent cost for inputs such as food.

An expert on foreign aid, Wolf was not against development programs in principle. Instead, he wanted a quid pro quo between government and population: "Rural improvement programs, in order to be of any benefit as an adjunct of counterinsurgency efforts, must be accompanied by efforts to exact *something in return* for whatever benefits and improvements are provided" (1965, p. 7, emphasis in original). The population would receive resources from the government in exchange for cooperation with government efforts to reduce the availability of those resources to insurgents.

At its core, Wolf's alternative theory (which has come to be called the cost/benefit, or coercion, theory) sought to apply RAND's systems analysis and econometric techniques to COIN. Insurgencies (and by extension counterinsurgencies) were viewed as systems and all COIN efforts should be evaluated in terms of how well they either raised the cost of inputs to the system or interfered with outputs (such as guerrilla fighters or terrorists). Populations were viewed as rational actors that would respond in more or less predictable ways to incentives and sanctions from the competing systems of insurgent and counterinsurgent. Ultimately, what mattered to both systems was not the population's *attitudes* but its *actions*. Wolf, along with fellow RAND analyst Nathan Leites, would further refine this theory throughout the remainder of the 1960s, culminating in Leites and Wolf's *Rebellion and Authority* (1970).

Although Leites and Wolf were perhaps the strongest proponents of this theory at RAND, they were not alone. Though not addressing theory explicitly, a RAND study of economic assistance to Vietnam in 1964 made points quite consonant with the cost/benefit theory (Zwick et al., 1964). It called for reorienting the emphasis of economic assistance away from the rural population generally, and instead attempting to expand economic opportunities for the urban population, which was more firmly under government control. It also argued, "In developing the rural program, benefits must be distributed more selectively. . . . The peasant is more likely to take an active part on the GVN [Government of Vietnam] side in defense of such a tangible stake for his family and community than out of abstract loyalty to a distant, little-understood central government" (Zwick et al., 1964, p. vii).

Others made similar arguments against HAM theory. One RAND analyst, in discussing criteria for success in COIN, stated, "Many authors regard economic growth as one of the criteria for winning. This is not listed here as necessary, though in most cases some economic betterment of the people is necessary for popular support of the government and its programs. . . . Popular support helps develop a government or contributes to its viability, but it may not be a necessary condition" (Farmer, 1964, pp. 2–3).

Non-RAND analysts also supported at least some of the arguments of cost/benefit theory. Most notably, scholar Samuel Popkin wrote on the cost/benefit calculations of Vietnamese peasants in a book titled *The Rational Peasant* (1979). While Popkin was uncomfortable with the implications of cost/benefit from a normative perspective, his work affirmed one of its key tenets.[6] However, even as cost/benefit theory gained support, some at RAND began to question its overemphasis on the purely material.

Critiques of Cost/Benefit: Ratcheted Escalation and Marginal Costs

The objections to the cost/benefit theory of COIN on other than normative grounds fell into two related categories. The first was what can be termed the *ratcheted escalation* problem. This refers to the problem posed by the interaction of escalation by both sides in a conflict. This interaction can change the nature of the conflict itself in ways that

---

[6]   Popkin was involved in field research in Vietnam and came to be a moderate critic of the war.

make de-escalation all but impossible. Thus, escalation in some cases could be said to exhibit the characteristics of a ratchet, which allows free movement in one direction (escalation) while restricting it in the opposite direction (de-escalation).

For example, during the Cold War, analysts believed that, durnig a conventional war in Europe, several possible escalatory mechanisms could lead one side to use nuclear weapons (see Posen, 1982). This use would probably begin at the tactical or theater nuclear level. Once this use happened, the other side would feel compelled to escalate to that level as well. Then both sides would be forced to consider escalating to the strategic nuclear level, while neither would consider de-escalating back to purely conventional conflict, as the nature of the war had changed. The war would either be terminated or escalate.

A similar dynamic of ratcheted escalation changing the nature of the conflict can be seen in COIN. In COIN, the problem is that repressive measures taken by the government in response to insurgency can actually stimulate insurgent activity. Constantin Melnik argued that violent repression could actually make insurgency stronger. Melnik, intimately involved in French COIN in Algeria, was not against the use of repression in itself. It was repression improperly applied that was the problem, as he argued:

> [I]t is necessary to eliminate the negative feelings on which the insurgency is based. *However, the use of force and violence runs the risk of increasing these same negative feelings.* An entire technique of violence must be elaborated and yet is not being taught in Western war colleges. (1964, p. 146, emphasis in original)

Cost/benefit theorists would respond that "negative feelings" are irrelevant; it is negative actions that matter. Albert Wohlstetter was one of the first to point out the problem with this argument. In comments on a draft of *Rebellion and Authority*, he notes:

> More important, an analysis that stresses very heavily making high the price to the population of supporting the rebels and that neglects the preferences of the population for goods and services (or for absolute and relative increases in income) might, in the limit, suggest reducing per capita so drastically that little would

be left over to buy the services of the rebels. . . . However, the support of people outside (your "X"), to say nothing of the people inside, might be affected by such drastic reductions in population income. Moreover they are bad in themselves and should be considered an item in the calculation. (1968b, pp. 2–3)

Essentially, Wohlstetter was arguing that while, at the extreme, sufficient repression could break any insurgency, it might not be possible to carry out. Soviet COIN in Central Asia and the Caucasus as well as British COIN in the Boer War had essentially followed cost/benefit theory to the limit successfully (see Baumann, 1993; and Pakenham, 1979). Yet those were different circumstances; democratic populations in the 1960s would not support the limits of repression. This had clearly been the case with the French in Algeria, where the increasing repression used against the population had agitated the Algerian population and turned many in metropolitan France against the war (see Horne, 1987).

Returning to the earlier analogy of escalation during the Cold War, it was as if the strategic nuclear level of escalation was unavailable. Both sides would be trapped, unable to escalate further but unable to de-escalate either. This, then, was the essence of the ratcheted escalation problem. If repression at a certain level were insufficient to subdue the insurgents, then it would become necessary to increase that repression. This could, in turn, increase insurgency as the population, under pressure, resisted. The COIN forces could then ratchet repression up further. Yet the ultimate limit of repression was not available to the COIN force of a modern democracy, so the escalation of repression might be stopped before it achieved its aim.[7] The COIN force would be trapped by the ratchet, having escalated but unable to make the final repressive effort needed to quell the insurgency.[8]

---

[7] Merom (2003) discusses both the benefits of and the limits on repression for democracies.

[8] There is a parallel here to the more general problem of escalation under conditions of limited war, which plagued the entire U.S. effort in Vietnam, both in COIN in South Vietnam and in bombing in North Vietnam.

It was therefore possible, even likely, that modern democracies using cost/benefit theory as a guide to COIN would find their efforts turned against them. Repression, while effective initially, could ultimately be self-defeating. RAND analysts likened this process to judo, in which the force of an attacker is redirected against the attacker. Melnik stated, "[T]he counterinsurgent resembles an old boxer, huge but awkward, who becomes the toy of a small and youthful judo artist. His hammer blows miss their mark or if they do not, his smaller adversary turns their force against him" (1964, p. 136). Daniel Ellsberg went further in developing this analogy, in an essay titled *Revolutionary Judo* (1970).

Ellsberg also noted the other, related effect that repressive efforts could have. By altering the population's preferences (which could initially be neutral or even favorable to the government), repressive measures could change the marginal cost of the inputs to the systems of insurgent and counterinsurgent that Wolf described. Ellsberg couched his argument in the language of *Rebellion and Authority* (P for population, R for rebellion, A for authority): "With new attitudes in P—then, with P providing more help for R, and less for A, for given inducement and effort by each—R could grow from its small beginnings, press A increasingly, perhaps win" (Ellsberg, 1970, p. 2).

The central point of Ellsberg's argument was that cost/benefit theory could not take preferences as a given. Cost/benefit theory assumed the population to be completely indifferent to insurgent and counterinsurgent, so whichever side provided the better set of incentives and disincentives would prevail. Both government and insurgent could "purchase" a given input for a marginal cost of x. Ellsberg contended that this preference assumption was incorrect; that government action could change this marginal cost of inputs so that insurgents would only have to pay x for an input while government might have to pay more for the same input. Thus, government repression that increased the cost of insurgent inputs in some ways (e.g., by expropriating crops) paradoxically could ultimately make inputs cheaper by altering preferences in the population.

Wohlstetter made similar comments on *Rebellion and Authority*, noting that both insurgents and counterinsurgents had to take care to use force in ways that did not undercut their claims to legitimacy (at least if the insurgents sought to replace the current regime with one of their own). Without legitimacy, there could never be a termination of repression and the costs associated with it. These costs could ultimately bankrupt even a powerful empire, if the gains from imperial holdings do not pay for the costs of retaining them (as Wolf et al. noted in the seminal RAND study *The Costs of the Soviet Empire*).[9] The British Empire, in its post–World War II COIN efforts, was forced to acknowledge this by allowing independence in Malaya and Kenya, and increasing autonomy for Northern Ireland.[10]

Wohlstetter also argued that preferences mattered and, moreover, that preferences in the population were heterogeneous, ranging from committed supporters of the government to committed supporters of the insurgents, with varying levels in between. Wolf, he notes, rightly argues that a small, highly committed minority can begin an insurgency. Yet insurgency can only be sustained if an additional portion of the population has at least some greater preference for the insurgents over the government (and, hence, lower marginal cost of inputs for insurgents).[11] Considering these preferences and their distribution, and undertaking actions that would move preferences toward, rather than away from, the government was critical for COIN.

---

[9]   See Wolf et al. (1983). This study excluded military costs (with the appropriate exception of the costs of Soviet COIN in Afghanistan) but not other forms of repression (e.g., Ministry of Internal Affairs, or Ministerstvo vnutrennykh del [MVD] and Committee for State Security, or Komitet gosudarstvennoi bezopasnosti [KGB] personnel stationed in the empire).

[10]   See Mockaitis (1990, 1995). The British admittedly took autonomy away from Northern Ireland as "the Troubles" got worse, but were ready to restore it (and even to give Northern Ireland independence if a majority of the population wanted it).

[11]   For a game-theoretic approach and empirical study on the role of heterogeneous preference in COIN, see Petersen (2001).

Moving COIN Theory Forward: Is Synthesis Possible?

The debate in COIN theory, to be clear, is not about whether preferences (HAM) or incentives/disincentives (cost/benefit) alone determine human behavior; rather, the question is which dominates the decisionmaking of individuals. This debate has been mirrored by a more general debate in the field of economics between neoclassical and behavioral economics. Neoclassical economists assume humans to be utility maximizers (as in cost/benefit theory of COIN), while behavioral economists attempt to probe empirical economic decisionmaking. Behavioral economists argue that humans, due to peculiarities of cognition, often violate the expectations of utility maximization assumed by neoclassical models.[12]

Decision theorist James March describes these two alternative models of decisionmaking as the "logic of consequence" and the "logic of appropriateness" (March and Heath, 1994). The logic of consequence evaluates decisions by looking forward to outcomes, rationally estimating probabilities of positive and negative results from an act. A decision is the answer to the question, "What will doing this get me?" The logic of appropriateness evaluates decisions by looking to rules that will relate the decision to the individual's identity. A decision is the answer to the question, "What should someone like me do?"

This author does not claim to have a definitive answer to the debate between the theories, but offers a few suggestions. In examining the debate between HAM and cost/benefit, it would appear that acknowledging that humans actually follow both logics simultaneously would be a good first step. Incentives clearly do matter to humans, driving many decisions in daily life. Yet preferences, particularly those that involve the legitimacy or illegitimacy of an action, quite obviously affect decisionmaking as well. The interaction of microlevel incentives with personal conceptions of identity and legitimacy probably provide the best guide to action.

For example, in Vietnam, both the Viet Cong (VC) and the Army of the Republic of Vietnam (ARVN) practiced conscription. A draftee

---

[12] For an excellent discussion of this debate, see Mullainathan and Thaler (2002).

for either side faced hardship, as well as possible injury and death. How would a draftee decide whom to serve, or in system terms, how much would the input of manpower cost the insurgent and counterinsurgent systems?

A quotation from one of the analytic products of the Viet Cong Motivation and Morale study provides insight into how the logics of consequence and appropriateness combined in the decision to opt for joining the VC:

> Numerous sources said that their decision to join the Front had been affected by the imminent or even remote prospect of being conscripted into the ARVN (and earlier, the French army). Thus, VC cadres often have been able to deflect youth receiving GVN draft notices into their own ranks. Here, they frequently hold out the attractive promise that a man's service in the VC will not take him away from his home hamlet or village, although in fact it often does.
>
> The VM [Viet Minh] earlier and the VC more recently have been able to play on widespread nationalist suspicions of the French and American roles in the war to arouse latent or overt fear of exploitation by foreigners. Closely entwined with this has been the propaganda claim that death may well attend military service but it is more glorious if suffered for the right cause; and moreover, it is more certain to come to a man who fights on the side of the exploitative, blundering foreign imperialists (Donnell, 1966, p. 79).

This illustrates the influence of both incentives/consequences (staying near home, less likely to be killed) and preferences/appropriateness (nationalist over foreign, death better in right cause) on the decision to join one side or the other.

By acknowledging that both logics are at work, rather than focusing on just one, both theory and the practical recommendations that follow from theory can be enhanced. In the case above, a recommendation to the South Vietnamese might have been to make service in the Regional and Popular Forces (RF/PF), the provincial and village militias, or both more attractive (e.g., increasing pay and providing better equipment) and an alternative to being drafted into the ARVN.

At the same time, accepting the need for the government to be seen as "a right cause" would lead to a recommendation about improving ARVN behavior toward the population.

In fact, both recommendations were made. The first recommendation was implemented to some extent after 1967, but the second was not (at least not effectively). The result was a "brittle" regime, one that was reasonably strong until highly stressed. The Thieu regime had eliminated much of the VC after the Tet Offensive and was providing a more attractive set of incentives (and disincentives) to many villagers than the VC were able to offer. The government had more or less successfully followed the recommendations of the cost/benefit theory, but without building sufficient legitimacy.[13] When stressed by conventional invasion in 1975, it fell apart.[14]

---

[13] See Popkin (1970) and Maranto and Tuchman (1992). Both articles discuss the incentives provided to peasants but acknowledge some role for legitimacy.

[14] The end of the Vietnam War remains hotly debated. Some argue that if the United States had continued to support South Vietnam in the 1970s and once again applied massive airpower as in 1972, the North Vietnamese would have again been halted. Others point out that, with the exception of a few elite units, the ARVN essentially routed, indicating a pervasive weakness in South Vietnamese political and social life. This author accepts this latter interpretation. The 1975 invasion, while massive, achieved results in excess of what even its planners expected to achieve as the Thieu regime and its security apparatus melted away. For the former interpretation, see Hosmer, Kellen, and Jenkins (1978). For the latter, see Duiker (1996, Chapter Twelve).

Figure 4.2
Joseph Zasloff and John Donnell, Whose Work on Insurgent Motivation
and Morale Illustrates the Need to Synthesize the Two Schools of
Counterinsurgency Theory, Pictured with Vietnamese Staff

SOURCE: Collection of Joseph Zasloff. Used with permission.
RAND *MG482-4.2*

CHAPTER FIVE

The Social Scientists' Wars: RAND and COIN Practice

In addition to work on the theoretical understanding of COIN, RAND conducted considerable research into the practice of counterinsurgency. This work, as alluded to earlier, ranged from seeking to develop more effective munitions for interdicting the Ho Chi Minh Trail in Laos to attempting to improve organizational structures for COIN. Given this breadth, this study is limited to four broad categories that appear to have particular relevance in the context of current (and probably future) COIN operations. These categories are organization of insurgents and counterinsurgents, border control systems, amnesty and reward programs, and pacification. The last category is particularly broad, and some would argue could encompass both organization and amnesty/reward.

Incidentally, the second category (border control) indicates that, contrary to the musings of Secretary of Defense Robert McNamara, not all of COIN is "the social scientist's war" (see Marquis, 2000, p. 79). Border security systems require extensive technical and system expertise. However, as will be discussed, even these concrete systems require an understanding of social and political factors.

Organization and COIN: Who Does What and How Would One Know?

One of the central elements of RAND's research on COIN was in the realm of organization. Many researchers and consultants at RAND had conducted groundbreaking research in the field of organization theory, so RAND was well qualified in this respect (see Leites, 1951; and Selznick, 1952). This effort encompassed research on both insurgent and counterinsurgent organization. In the former, RAND sought to understand more than just the conventional (though sometimes controversial) enemy order of battle. It sought to develop a picture of the political and social construction of insurgent organization, which many considered to be its chief strength. Similarly, RAND analysts sought to develop better metrics than the invidious "body count" for measuring progress against insurgent organization. In terms of counterinsurgent organization, one of the main findings of RAND research was that the normal division of labor between bureaucracies and the standard operating procedures of most government organizations are inadequate to cope with COIN. The research focused on why this was the case and how successful COIN efforts overcame this handicap.

Insurgent Organization

RAND extensively investigated the organization of the Viet Cong, in as great detail as was possible using interviews with captured and surrendered personnel, captured documents, intelligence reports, and travel to Vietnam. The concept of insurgent organization employed by RAND researchers was much broader than compiling organization charts and counting enemy guerrillas. Instead, as one report noted, "Central to the study is the treatment of the Viet Cong movement as a 'system,' which implies regularly interacting or interdependent elements forming a unified whole" (Elliott and Stewart, 1969, p. ix).

The view of the "system" that emerged from RAND's efforts was one of an insurgent movement with many elements, dominated by a central but diffuse set of ideologies. The main elements of the insurgent movement were the Communist Party (which had several names), the Liberation Army (which had several components in itself), and the NLF civilian organization. The central ideologies of the insurgency were nationalism, anticolonialism, and social justice. Despite popular perception, most Liberation Army foot soldiers and lower-level members of the NLF knew little about communism (though they might be able to parrot some slogans). Only the Communist Party cadre was deeply imbued with communist thought and seldom used it to recruit and motivate troops.

This system was both strong and cumbersome. The Liberation Army, for example, was composed of Main Force, Regional Force, and Local Force units. The VC sought to maintain balance between the three types of forces as they were mutually supporting. Main Force units, which conducted major offensives, needed the other two as sources of future replacements, and to provide intelligence and other resources. The system as a whole needed the Regional and Local Forces to enforce the edicts of the party and protect political cadres. The Local Forces, in turn, needed the Main and Regional Forces to help shield them from major government attacks. The three had to be balanced as much as possible, leading to difficult resource allocation problems.

More important, perhaps, than the organizational relationships between the Party and the Army, or among the three elements of the Army, was the Viet Cong's emphasis on self-criticism, after-action review, and organizational learning. Complementing this focus was a willingness to absorb lessons provided from external sources or examples, to experiment with tactics and doctrine, and then to disseminate successful results widely. This ethos was inculcated by both Party and Army discipline, and led to notable organizational success in adapting to challenges posed by COIN operations (see Anderson, Arnsten, and Averch, 1967, esp. pp. 52–54).

As an example, the introduction of both helicopters and armored personnel carriers (APCs) to the conflict in the early 1960s was a huge problem for the VC. APCs rendered government forces nearly invulnerable to the small arms of the VC, and helicopters gave government forces unmatched mobility and firepower in even the most remote sections of Vietnam. The VC was initially unable to cope with either technological advantage, and suffered significantly.

In response, the Liberation Army began a program to design ways to neutralize both systems. For helicopters, it drew lessons from an Algerian officer who had fought helicopters, performed experiments of its own, then created widely distributed manuals with tables for gun-laying. Similarly, the VC countered APCs by developing techniques to suppress the vehicle's gunner then use Molotov cocktails or grenades against it. They also acquired more heavy weapons and became adept at creating antivehicle obstacles (see Anderson, Arnsten, and Averch, 1967, pp. 54–58).

The success of this organizational learning became apparent in January 1963, in what came to be called the Battle of Ap Bac. ARVN heliborne forces supported by APCs sought to engage what they thought was a relatively small VC unit in a Mekong Delta village south of Saigon. They encountered a well-prepared VC force that damaged all but one of the 15 helicopters, downing five. The APCs were unable to make progress against the defenses either, as withering fire continually killed or disabled the machine gunners (see Sheehan, 1989, Chapter Three).

RAND research also included assessments of the VC cadres, logistics, and tactics used during the Tet Offensive, and other subjects (see, among others, Gurtov, 1967; and Pohle, 1969). At the grainiest level of analysis, RAND translated and assessed a full set of captured documents from an elite sapper unit (see Elliott and Elliott, 1969a, 1969b, 1969c, 1969d, 1969e). All of this research centered on understanding how the VC system operated and converted inputs to outputs. The conclusion to which many analysts came was reflected in one study's thoughtful and sobering indictment of the U.S. attitude toward COIN:

> Whether the Viet Cong can adapt to the U.S. presence is a question for argument. Our study does not suffice for a finding on this question. . . . What we can say is that the Viet Cong organization is designed to react by carefully observing and analyzing U.S. behavior and, noting any weak points, modifying its own behavior accordingly. Our usual concept of insurgency is that of an automatic three-phase process. Counterinsurgency programs have been built around this distinction. Planning and programming for insurgency, as does strategic nuclear planning and programming, should adopt the concept of the enemy as a learning, adapting, reacting organization (Anderson, Arnsten, and Averch, 1967, pp. xiii–xiv).

Indicators in COIN

RAND also conducted some research both developing and evaluating indicators and metrics in COIN. This was of central importance to COIN efforts, as metrics for COIN are less intuitive than many conventional measures of progress in warfare. In conventional warfare, the objective is generally the destruction of enemy capability to wage war and the seizure or defense of territory. Metrics for measuring success such as the movement of the battle lines (or fronts), number of enemy units destroyed, or enemy factories rendered inoperative are fairly easy to generate and understand.

In COIN, the intimate relationship of the political, social, economic, and military factors of the war makes metrics much harder to generate. If one subscribes to HAM theory, how does one measure the population's support for government or insurgent? If one subscribes to cost/benefit theory, how does one measure and optimize the effects of carrots and sticks? Conventional warfare metrics are of little use in this situation. Territory held is irrelevant if the real "center of gravity" is the population. Number of enemy killed can be useful in some cases, but highly misleading in others. In Malaya, the British knowledge of the insurgent organization, combined with the isolation of the insurgents, meant that a "body count" of insurgents killed was a reasonable metric. In Vietnam, the U.S. use of a "body count" was highly deceptive, as the insurgents were not isolated, having access to both external support and the population.

As an alternative, analysts in Vietnam created a new set of metrics, collectively known as the Hamlet Evaluation System (HES). HES was developed by CIA analysts (with military input) to provide a means of measuring the progress of the somewhat nebulous concept of pacification. It consisted of 18 indicators grouped into six major categories. Each indicator was scored for each hamlet (a small subset of a village) on a scale of 1 to 5 (or A to E), and each category was then given a "confidence rating" by the assessor based on how accurate he believed the scores to be (see George W. Allen, 2001, pp. 219–228; and Komer, 1970, pp. 198–203).

HES became one of the most contentious metrics of the Vietnam War. The problem was that the aggregate scores of hundreds of villages were used to measure progress in the war as a whole. Prior to the Tet Offensive of 1968, the HES scores had been showing an upward trend, reinforcing the belief of many that the war was being won. After Tet, many came to believe the measure was worthless.

RAND was asked to evaluate HES and make suggestions for improving it. In his analysis of HES in 1968, Anders Sweetland began by noting:

> Thus far, our search for a person who feels neutral about the HES has been fruitless. People are either for it or against it, with the "agins" outnumbering the field six to one. No measure in the theater has been so thoroughly damned. Certainly no measure has been so thoroughly misunderstood (p. 1).

He went on to discuss the strengths and limitations of HES. HES appeared to be a reliable way to get an overall sense of whether a given hamlet was making progress in pacification or not. However, making this the overall measure of the progress of the highly complicated war was inappropriate and misleading. Sweetland found HES to be a reasonably reliable set of metrics, if one accepted that no "objective" criteria for measuring pacification existed.

Sweetland made further recommendations for expanding HES with additional metrics. These metrics were VC taxation, VC recruitment, and a "freedom of speech" metric. The ability to speak freely was particularly important, and accorded with the belief of many that the willingness of a population to provide information both on the failures of government as well as on the insurgents was an excellent measure of pacification. Sweetland commented, "Our suspicion is that an adequate representation of the willingness to speak freely would be the best possible single index of pacification" (1968, p. 8).

COIN Organization

RAND also undertook extensive study of the organization of governments for COIN. This set of research can most accurately be summed up as understanding how to prevent bureaucracy from "doing its thing." The central finding was that government agencies, both civilian and military, are generally not well structured for COIN. COIN falls between the normal function of civilian agencies for peacetime aid and development and the normal function of militaries for high-intensity conflict. Further, the intimate connection of the political and military in COIN requires careful coordination of the civilian agencies with the military.

One early RAND publication to note the importance of organization and the coordination of political and military activity was *Pacification in Algeria* (Galula, 1963, 2006). In this study, French Col. David Galula describes his campaign against insurgents east of Algiers. Galula firmly believed in the supremacy of the political and civil over the military in COIN, and called for the two to be joined in a unified command structure, either a committee or a unified staff. Galula also felt that conventional armies would have to transform both their force structure and mindset in order to adapt successfully to COIN.[1]

In addition to Galula, one of the most notable RAND authors on this subject was Robert "Blowtorch Bob" Komer (shown discussing Vietnam with President Johnson in Figure 5.1).[2] Komer served as Deputy Commander for Civil Operations and Revolutionary Development Support (DEPCORDS), Military Assistance Command Vietnam (MACV). CORDS was intended to coordinate all nonmilitary aspects of the COIN effort in Vietnam. In *Bureaucracy Does Its Thing*, Komer (1972a) discussed the pitfalls of using institutions to perform tasks other than those for which they were intended and the problems of not coordinating the civil and military elements of COIN.

In the case of the institutions that carried out COIN, Komer argues that the U.S. military carried out its institutional repertoire through firepower-intensive "search-and-destroy" missions intended to attrite the VC and North Vietnamese personnel. Similarly, the State

---

[1] These points were emphasized in Galula's book *Counterinsurgency Warfare*, which was based on his RAND work (see Galula, 1964, pp. 87–96).

[2] Komer's nickname referenced his combination of penetrating intellect and bruising style of bureaucratic combat, honed by service in the Army and CIA as well as Harvard Business School.

Figure 5.1
Robert Komer, DEPCORDS, and President Lyndon Johnson

SOURCE: Lyndon Baines Johnson Library photo by Yoichi R. Okamoto.
RAND *MG482-5.1*

Department dealt with the government of South Vietnam as if it were any other government, despite its instability and the massive infusion of American personnel and capital into the country. The U.S. Agency for International Development (USAID) is also critiqued, though less so, for providing aid through its normal, peacetime methods rather than generating new ones to meet the rapid pace of war (see Komer, 1972a, pp. 37–63; see also Selznick, 1952, pp. 56–65).

Komer also criticized the lack of unified management of COIN in Vietnam. He contrasted U.S. COIN management with that of the British in Malaya (see Komer, 1972b; see also Sunderland, 1964a). The United States gave significant autonomy to each civilian agency and the military, with the result for COIN that "below Presidential level everybody and nobody was responsible for coping with it in the round" (Komer, 1972a, p. 75).

Former CIA officer Douglas Blaufarb came to the same conclusions on the importance of unified management in COIN. As a RAND analyst, Blaufarb assessed two U.S.-supported COIN efforts with which he was associated in Laos and Thailand (Blaufarb, 1972a, 1972b). In the Thai effort, he concluded that good policies had been poorly implemented, in large part due to the lack of organization. In contrast, the resource-constrained U.S. effort to support COIN in Laos was relatively successful due to good management. Blaufarb notes, "However one approaches the organization of the unconventional war in Laos, one comes back to the importance of unified field management as the key to the matter" (Blaufarb, 1972a, p. 90).

Brian Jenkins leveled similar criticisms against the U.S. COIN effort in Vietnam, but focused more on the military element of COIN. Jenkins' *The Unchangeable War* (1970a) argued that the U.S. Army was designed around "total war" in central Europe, and was therefore unwilling, and to some extent unable, to adapt to the war in Vietnam (see also Canby, Jenkins, and Rainey, 1970). Steve Hosmer (1990) amplified these concerns in a later monograph calling for the Army to develop a dedicated COIN cadre and training program. He pointed out that in the future the United States might face insurgency in the Third World following successful conventional operations.

RAND analyst Francis "Bing" West focused on assessing Marine efforts to conduct smaller and more targeted COIN efforts. One program, the Combined Action Platoon (CAP), supported the Popular Force militias in the villages through *encadrement* with small units of Marines (West, 1969a, 1985). Figure 5.2 shows one such unit. Another program used intensive, small-unit patrolling and reconnaissance to locate insurgents away from populated areas in order to use U.S. firepower effectively (West, 1969b). West argued that these innovations did not receive the serious attention they deserved from the more conventionally minded leadership of the military.

After Vietnam, Bruce Hoffman made similar observations on the critical importance of organization for COIN. In analyzing the development of British and Rhodesian responses to COIN, he concluded that coordination between the police, civil administration, and military down to the tactical level is almost a prerequisite for success.

Similarly, small unit operations and careful intelligence work are needed rather than the typical firepower-intensive conventional response (see Hoffman, Taw, and Arnold, 1991; and Hoffman and Taw, 1991). Hoffman (2004) makes similar recommendations about COIN in Iraq.

Figure 5.2
A Marine Captain Inspecting a Combined Action Unit That Fully Integrated
Vietnamese and U.S. Personnel at the Squad Level

SOURCE: Shulimson and Johnson (1965).
RAND *MG482-5.2*

Amnesty and Reward: Catching More Flies with Honey

The second major category of RAND research on COIN practice examined the effectiveness of amnesty programs and the related use of rewards as an incentive for surrender or informing on insurgents.[3] Both amnesty and reward were potentially cost-effective programs, as even expensive rewards were often more efficient at removing enemy combatants than were large military actions. More importantly, amnesty made surrender a potentially attractive option, reducing the need for a "fight-to-the-finish."

David Galula, though not specifically discussing amnesty and reward, points to the importance of lenience and good treatment of prisoners whenever possible. He noted, "In the best camps, efforts were made to sift the tough prisoners from the soft; where it was not done, the camps became schools for rebel cadres" (Galula, 1963, p. 313). He also argued that leniency should be based on willingness to confess all previous offenses and cooperate with the government in the future. This conditional forgiveness is the heart of any amnesty program, even if it is not specifically named as such.

Galula, who observed Indochina from an attaché posting in Hong Kong and did not directly participate in the urban "Battle of Algiers" in 1956–1958, was not a proponent of torture. Recognizing the need for arrests and detention, he nonetheless argued, "The main concern of the counterinsurgent . . . is to minimize the possible adverse effects produced on the population by the arrests" (Galula, 1964, p. 127). In this, he differed significantly from many of his fellow French COIN practitioners, including Roger Trinquier and Paul Aussaresses. Veterans of the ferocious Indochina conflict, Trinquier and Aussaresses used torture and summary execution to end brutally and quickly the urban terrorist campaign of the Front de Liberation Nationale (FLN) (see Trinquier, 1964; and Aussaresses, 2002). However, they were then forced to confront the corrosive effects of torture on support for the COIN effort among the populations of both Algeria and France. This

---

[3]   Some of the RAND research on rewards in COIN remains classified. A recent overview and analysis of the rewards program in Malaya is Ramakrishna (2002).

corrosion also affected the entire French Army and amplified the tensions that would lead to coup attempts, the terrorist Organisation de l'Armée Secrète (OAS), and the end of France's Fourth Republic. Even the heroic Marcel Bigeard, who scrupulously avoided using torture even as he effectively battled the FLN in both Algiers and the countryside, felt sullied by the use of torture and summary execution.[4]

In addition to other research on rewards in Malaya and the treatment of detainees in Algeria, the Viet Cong Motivation and Morale Study examined the "Chieu Hoi" (loosely translated as "Open Arms") amnesty program in Vietnam. Chieu Hoi offered amnesty to VC defectors, and, after interrogation and some reeducation efforts at a Chieu Hoi center, tried to reintegrate them into South Vietnamese society.

In a 1966 study of Chieu Hoi, RAND researchers argued that while Chieu Hoi was far from decisive in influencing VC to defect, it did make a contribution. Many of the defectors (referred to as "ralliers" or "Hoi Chanh") cited knowledge of Chieu Hoi as an influence in the decision to leave the VC. Often they would ask family members to verify that the Chieu Hoi program was legitimate and that they would not be mistreated. Once reassured, they would leave the ranks, generally due to the hardships imposed by war rather than by any political conversion to the cause of South Vietnam (Carrier and Thomson, 1966). Figure 5.3 shows a participant in the Chieu Hoi amnesty program with members of his former unit.

One of the major problems of Chieu Hoi was the lack of status and resources accorded it, a problem with many nonmilitary efforts in Vietnam. Many in the South Vietnamese government found it distasteful, if not foolish, to reward former enemies. However, Chieu Hoi was eventually given the status of a full ministry in the South Vietnamese government with support from U.S. agencies. In its peak year, 1969, Chieu Hoi claimed over 47,000 ralliers at a per capita cost of $350 (roughly $1,875 in 2005 dollars) (Koch, 1973, pp. 46–50).

----

[4] Bigeard, a veteran of both Indochina and Algeria, is not well known in the United States, both because he wrote very little of his experiences until relatively recently and due to the lack of translation of those works into English. He was nonetheless one of the major French

Despite this success, Chieu Hoi had flaws that were never corrected. The most serious was the lack of follow-up on ralliers. Once they left the Chieu Hoi centers, little was done to track them or aid their reintegration into South Vietnam. Ralliers could be re-recruited by the VC, leading some to argue that Chieu Hoi was potentially nothing more than a rest-and-recreation program for the insurgents. Later efforts were made to correct this with improved tracking, but not until

Figure 5.3
A Participant in the Chieu Hoi Amnesty Program (in White Shirt) Posing with Captured Members of His Former Unit

SOURCE: Photograph VA000318, 1967, Douglas Pike Photograph Collection, The Vietnam Archive, Texas Tech University. Used with permission.
RAND *MG482-5.3*

---

practitioners of COIN. See, among others, Bigeard (1994, 1995, 1997). This author thanks Colin Jackson, whose knowledge of both French COIN and the French language far surpasses his own, for instruction on Bigeard.

very late in the war. Other weaknesses included the lack of resources, ineffective political reeducation, and continuing administrative weakness (see Koch, 1973, pp. 28–56, 107–108; see also Pye, 1966; and Simulmatics Corporation, 1967).

Another serious criticism leveled at the program was that it never attracted any ralliers above the lowest echelon of the VC (Koch, 1973, p. 108). The higher-level cadres of the South and the personnel of the North Vietnamese Army appeared almost immune to Chieu Hoi appeals. Yet Bob Komer, a major supporter of Chieu Hoi noted, "Even if half the Hoi Chanh who came in were really low level part-time porters, minor members of front organizations or plain farmers, it was still one of the most successful little programs in Vietnam. . . . It was ridiculously inexpensive and thus highly cost-effective" (Komer, 1970, p. 172).

Komer was similarly positive in his assessment of reward programs for surrender or information. In discussing the British COIN effort in Malaya, he argued, "The heart of the government's psychological warfare was its rewards-for-surrender program." He noted that these rewards were extremely lucrative, with even an ordinary soldier meriting $875 (on the order of $6,500 in 2005 dollars), while a platoon leader was worth $2,300 (roughly $17,000 in 2005 dollars) and a province secretary a princely $16,000 (over $110,000 in 2005 dollars). Providing information leading to the capture or killing of insurgents was worth approximately 75 percent of their surrender value and was cumulative. So informing on an insurgent platoon could lead to a payout equivalent to over $100,000 (in 2005 dollars) (Komer, 1972b, pp. 72–74).

Komer was also quick to note that while the high value of rewards was important to success, the ability to protect informants and surrendered enemy personnel was critical:

> Above a certain level the amount of money was often less important than the defector or informer's estimate of which side could protect him or hide him better from the other. Until the government could provide a defector or informer the protection he needed, the program got nowhere. But once it could do so—and make this clear to the insurgents—the program not only neutral-

ized a large number of insurgents who might otherwise have continued fighting, but it also provided Special Branch with a large flow of intelligence (full cooperation with the police being the price of the reward) (1972b, p. 74).

The obvious parallel is the U.S. Witness Protection Program, which seeks to guarantee the survival of those who inform on organized crime. Like Chieu Hoi, some were uncomfortable with protecting and rewarding those who had previously been enemies. Yet the program appeared to be somewhat effective in concert with other measures that put pressure on insurgents.

Border Security: Morice and McNamara: A Tale of Two Lines

RAND researchers noted the importance of cross-border sanctuary and supply to many insurgent organizations. Indeed, with few exceptions (perhaps most notably Cuba), successful insurgencies have been able to obtain aid and comfort from outside sources. Conversely, successful COIN operations appeared easier in isolated battlefields (Malaya, for example).

The question then became one of how to isolate the battlefield, and one possible answer was attempting to seal the border against insurgents. As a result, RAND did considerable work on anti-infiltration systems in Vietnam. First, researchers examined French efforts to seal the Algerian borders against insurgent infiltration, an effort that came to be called the Morice Line (after French Minister of Defense Andre Morice). Second, RAND evaluated proposals and concepts for possible systems to seal the Vietnamese borders with North Vietnam and Laos, some of which was later referred to as the McNamara Line (after U.S. Secretary of Defense Robert McNamara).

The Morice Line actually consisted of several border security systems in both the east and west of Algeria. The insurgents had established a considerable presence across the borders in Tunisia and Morocco, and were able to infiltrate sizable formations into Algeria almost at will. Beginning in 1956, the French began erecting barriers to at least make border crossing more difficult. Despite the allusion to the Maginot Line fortifications, the barriers in Algeria were instead interlocking fences (some electrified), minefields, lighting, and patrols. Combined with a variety of sensors, including ground surveillance radar, the barrier system was designed to impede and warn, rather than to prevent actual infiltration. However, by slowing the border crossing while warning the French that it was taking place, mobile reserve troops and indirect fire (air and artillery) could be brought to bear on insurgents very effectively.[5]

The effectiveness of the system, once fully emplaced, was nothing short of phenomenal. One author claims, "During the second half of 1960, only 40 men and 40 rifles were able to enter Algeria" (Melnik, 1964, p. 171). Even if this is an overstatement, the barrier system nonetheless reduced infiltration very significantly. This effectiveness did not come cheaply, as the mobile reserve eventually comprised 40,000 soldiers, apart from the considerable cost of the barriers themselves. However, both French civilians like Melnik and military practitioners like Galula supported the effort (see Melnik, 1964, pp. 170–173; and Galula, 1963, p. 97).

Using Algeria as an example, RAND researchers began exploring the utility of implementing a border-control system in Vietnam in the early 1960s. Researchers explored myriad options, including enhancing existing border surveillance, using air interdiction of enemy supply routes, constructing strong points along the border, and building a physical barrier system. The somewhat limited personnel and funds available before 1965 prevented any major border security system from being implemented.

This effort received further impetus from a summer study by the scientific advisers of the JASON Group in 1966. The JASON members proposed a barrier system that would incorporate advanced and automated sensor systems to limit infiltration. Secretary of Defense McNamara urged the military to implement this system (hence the

---

[5] Significant amounts of RAND research on border security remains classified or otherwise restricted. For an overview of the Morice Line, see Melnik (1964, pp. 170–173) and Horne (1978).

name McNamara Line), which was done on a limited basis along the border with North Vietnam. At the same time, the U.S. Air Force conducted an ongoing effort to interdict insurgent supplies and reinforcements along the Ho Chi Minh Trail through Laos. Ultimately, neither of these efforts stemmed the tide of infiltration, which increased as the war continued.[6] Figure 5.4 shows Nakhon Phanom Royal Thai Air Force Base, home of the infiltration surveillance center that monitored sensors along the Ho Chi Minh Trail.

RAND's conclusions on the importance of border security echoed those of the French earlier. After extensive computer modeling of infiltration, one study commented, *"In the absence of a border security system that at least hinders* or deters the enemy from determining freely his desired infiltration rates, no model solution leads to conflict termination"* (Schilling, 1970, p. 59, emphasis in original). Another study in 1971 argued that enhanced border surveillance combined with a strong-point system for staffed patrols would be ideal to limit infiltration from a cost-effectiveness perspective (Weiner and Schaffer, 1971). Ultimately, a major anti-infiltration system was never attempted in Vietnam, and RAND did little to explore border security for COIN after the end of the conflict.

---

[6] For an overview of the JASON study and the McNamara Line, see Twomey (1999).

Figure 5.4
Nakhon Phanom Royal Thai Air Force Base

SOURCE: Photograph VA044030, 01 August 1975, Robert A. Goode Collection,
The Vietnam Archive, Texas Tech University. Used with permission.
RAND *MG482-5.4*

Pacification: All Politics Is Local

As noted earlier, the term *pacification* is a broad and fairly vague term.
Here it will be used to mean the combination of security and development in a given unit of political administration (e.g., village, neighborhood, province). The two are intimately related, as development
without security is hostage to insurgents and security without development provides little (though some) incentive to support the government. Further, efforts to provide one can potentially help or hinder the
other.

RAND research on these topics acknowledged this interrelationship explicitly, though it acknowledged that how the relationship works is often unclear (see Heymann, 1969a, 1969b). However, one conclusion that appears to be commonly valid is, in the words of former Speaker of the House Tip O'Neill, "all politics is local." In COIN, it is not grand plans for nationwide infrastructure or overall economic growth that matter most. Nor is it the aggregate number of divisions produced in a local army that matters.

Instead, pacification is best thought of as a massively enhanced version of the "community policing" technique that emerged in the 1970s (encouraged in part by RAND research).[7] Community policing is centered on a broad concept of problem solving by law enforcement officers working in an area that is well-defined and limited in scale, with sensitivity to geographic, ethnic, and other boundaries. Patrol officers form a bond of trust with local residents, who get to know them as more than a uniform. The police work with local groups, businesses, churches, and the like to address the concerns and problems of the neighborhood.

Pacification is simply an expansion of this concept to include greater development and security assistance. For example, in Malaya, a Rural Industrial Development Authority (RIDA) was initiated to provide a means to finance locally initiated development projects (Komer, 1972b, p. 62). Similar measures have been successfully undertaken elsewhere, including the Philippines under Magsaysay.

This approach to development is also supported by both theories of COIN, proposed earlier. Local development gives communities a stake in the government as well as a voice. The RAND study on development in Vietnam advocating this approach noted, "[T]he peasant is given a personal stake in accepting and defending GVN jurisdiction over his locality. He is not expected to act of loyalty to the government, but in defense of a better life" (Zwick et al., 1964, p. 45). Of course, the government that successfully provides this better life stands a better chance of eventually winning citizens' loyalty.

---

[7] See Community Policing Consortium (1994). The RAND research underpinning much of this concept is Greenwood and Petersilia (1975) and Greenwood, Chaiken, et al. (1975).

In parallel to development, a local security force is needed to protect citizens. This is generally a paramilitary or militia, in the best sense of those words: citizens who are willing to be trained with weapons and give some of their time to protect their homes. Perhaps the kindest analogy is to the concept of the National Guard in the United States, which hearkens back to the "Minute Men" of the Revolutionary War. In Vietnam, as discussed earlier, this was the role of the Popular Forces, the Civilian Irregular Defense Groups, and the People's Self Defense Forces (Komer, 1970, pp. 106–108, 184–185). In Algeria, this role was played in large part by the forces devoted to *quadrillage*.[8]

This is not to say that a national army and a national development plan are not needed. National security and development are more than just aggregations of local security and development. Infrastructure connecting communities, for example, is a national concern from both an economic and security perspective. As DEPCORDS, Komer stressed the protection and development of roads and waterways as part of his efforts, which he justified on both economic and military grounds (Komer, 1970, pp. 122–126).

Other national measures in support of pacification include a census and national identification system. Without them, any form of tracking or investigation into insurgent activity is significantly more difficult. In Vietnam, the census was combined with a program to obtain information from peasants by allowing them to note any "grievances" they had (Komer, 1970, pp. 143, 166). In Malaya, the census and identification system became the basis for a massive program of resettlement and food control that allowed the government to deprive the insurgents of badly needed supplies (Komer, 1972b, pp. 53–54; and Sunderland, 1964b).

---

[8]   Melnik (1964, pp. 173–179). The forces devoted to *quadrillage* were mostly regular troops rather than locals, which was perhaps not ideal, but the general emphasis on area security was productive.

Figure 5.5
The Vietnamese Civil Guard, an Early Paramilitary Dedicated to Providing Local Security for COIN

SOURCE: Collins (1991).
RAND *MG482-5.5*

CHAPTER SIX

COIN Old and New

The body of RAND research on COIN suggests several practices and techniques for current COIN. Exploiting these practices would help the United States avoid further delay in its attempts to develop solutions for Iraq and Afghanistan, as well as for future COIN efforts. The recommendations that follow are, admittedly, subject to debate and in many cases will require further research on the specific insurgent environments.

Two major caveats are in order as well. First, no "silver bullet" solution to COIN exists. At best, the following recommendations can each make a substantial contribution to the COIN effort, and perhaps together bring the effort to a successful conclusion. Second, virtually all previous COIN campaigns have, in some sense, been products of the Cold War. Both the campaigns and research based on them were inevitably colored by the geopolitical context, which is today quite different. The full effects of this change on COIN are unclear at present.[1]

What is clear is that, unlike during the Cold War, COIN is no longer a sideshow to the main challenge faced by those charged with formulating and executing U.S. grand strategy. There is no longer a Central Front along the inter-German border that demands the bulk of civilian and military attention. The new Central Front in the cur-

---

[1] One major change is the increased availability of personal weapons in the world following the emptying of the Warsaw Pact arsenals in the 1990s. Insurgents who might previously have had to manufacture their own crude weapons or to capture them can often arm themselves very well from the beginning. The Kosovo Liberation Army, for example, was greatly aided by the near-collapse of Albania and the resulting fire-sale of weapons.

rent struggle against terrorists of global reach, to the extent that there is one, is COIN in Iraq and Afghanistan. One need not accept all of the predicted consequences of defeat enumerated in the recently released *National Strategy for Victory in Iraq* to realize the critical importance of current and future COIN to U.S. security (NSC, 2005, pp. 5–6).

Organizing for COIN: Breaking the Interagency Phalanx

The first set of recommendations is on the organization of U.S. forces for COIN. These variables, unlike many others in COIN, are fully in the control of the United States and should be fully implemented. Resistance will be, as Komer suggests, from bureaucracies, civilian and military, that have no interest in performing for COIN in a way inconsistent with their values and practices. It is worth noting that, according to one source, Komer's *Bureaucracy Does Its Thing* is circulating in Baghdad and is considered to be the best guide to the situation there (see Packer, 2005, pp. 442–443). Breaking the bureaucratic phalanx of "business as usual" should be paramount.

Above all other things, a unified civilian and military structure should be established for all COIN efforts. This should probably take the form of councils or staffs, like the British had in Malaya, in which military officers, civilian administrators, local government officials, and police all are full participants. These councils should extend down to the lower levels of military and civilian administrations. At the very top should be a senior official with full power over both the military and civilian aspects of COIN.

This proposal is far-reaching in its implications. It would, for example, mean that no military activity (other than immediate self-defense) could be initiated without approval by the council. The same would be true of police operations, reconstruction, and intelligence gathering.

One can imagine the howls of protest from the U.S. military and, perhaps to a lesser extent, the intelligence community. War by committee is anathema in high-intensity conflict, where shock, speed, and surprise are generally paramount. This is not the case in much of COIN, where consistency and close coordination are more important. Organization for COIN requires integrating all elements as tightly as possible; even if this might entail the loss of some short-term *efficiency*, it will be more than compensated for by gains in long-term *effectiveness*.[2]

Some efforts have already been made to move in this direction. The *National Strategy for Victory in Iraq* has a section devoted to "Organization for Victory." This section indicates both the complexity of the task (eight pillars of strategy, each incorporating all elements of national power along multiple lines of action) and the recognition of the importance of organization for such a wide-ranging effort. It further states that the organization will consist of an interagency working group for each pillar of the strategy, combined with weekly meetings of senior U.S. government officials (NSC, 2005, pp. 25–26).

While an encouraging step in the right direction, this organization is insufficient. The interagency process, while good for discussion and generating options for decision, is woefully inadequate for execution. This is the essence of Komer's critique of the Vietnam effort, and has been reiterated as recently as late 2004 by then Vice-Chairman (now Chairman) of the Joint Chiefs of Staff Gen. Peter Pace.[3] Each participant in the interagency group is not ultimately responsible to the group but to his or her own agency. After the interagency group makes decisions, the execution is left to the agencies themselves, which may or may not coordinate, particularly at lower levels in each agency. Weekly meetings by senior leadership, while important, will not be able to make up for this shortfall in execution.

Fortunately, another, better model has also been implemented in certain areas. In both Afghanistan and, more recently, Iraq, the Provincial Reconstruction Team (PRT) has been introduced as a way

---

[2] Americans sometimes conflate efficiency and effectiveness. Efficiency is the amount of output from a system for given input; effectiveness is how well that output produces the desired result.

[3] See Komer (1972a) and Garamone (2004). For a longer discussion of interagency interactions in Iraq, see Schnaubelt (2005–2006).

Figure 6.1
U.S. Military Officers and the Afghan Provincial Governor Inaugurating a
Provincial Reconstruction Team in 2004

SOURCE: Photo by Sgt. Stephanie L. Carl.
RAND *MG482-6.1*

to coordinate the various elements of the U.S. government (see, among others, McNerney, 2005–2006; Gall, 2003; and Tomlinson, 2005). These teams include military personnel, State Department officials, development experts, and local government representatives. These teams are intended to accomplish the dual missions of security and development/reconstruction vital to successful COIN efforts. Figure 6.1 shows an inauguration of a PRT.

While an excellent initial innovation, the PRTs need both addition and revision. As the name implies, PRTs operate at the province level. Ideally, similarly organized village or neighborhood teams would operate below them. Major urban areas might, in fact, need a separate organization from the PRT—a city reconstruction team—in order to avoid overwhelming any one PRT with responsibility.

Above the PRT level should be a National Reconstruction Team, headed by a single individual with final authority (apart from the

President) over all U.S. decisions made concerning Iraq. Currently, Gen. George Casey and Ambassador Zalmay Khalilzad are co-equal in Iraq, with USCENTCOM Commander Gen. John Abizaid also in the background. While perhaps adequate at the moment, as Casey, Khalilzad, and Abizaid appear to get along reasonably well, it is not a good model for continuing operations or future operations. This model is far too personality-dependent. Lt. Gen. Ricardo Sanchez and Ambassador L. Paul Bremer, Casey and Khalilzad's predecessors in Iraq, apparently did not get along well, with a resulting loss in effectiveness (see Packer, 2005, pp. 304–305, 324–327). COIN organization should attempt to minimize this dependence on personality by having a final and ultimate decisionmaker.

The National Reconstruction Team should also include senior Iraqi leaders. This could lead to a standoff between the U.S. and Iraqi governments over certain courses of action, the amnesty recommended below being but one of many potentially contentious issues. Nevertheless, at the very least, the U.S. government would be "speaking with one voice" to the Iraqi leadership, an improvement over both the current arrangement in Iraq as well as previous COIN campaigns such as Vietnam.

The current organizational structure, perhaps not coincidentally, is very similar to the one the United States adopted in Vietnam, with the Ambassador and the Commander, U.S. Military Assistance Command, Vietnam, coequal and dominant in their respective spheres, and the U.S. Pacific Command (USPACOM) Commander in the background.[4] This organizational arrangement, for reasons of bureaucratic politics, appears to be the default status for major COIN operations conducted by the United States. Instead of allowing politics to triumph over good organization, the ambassador, as the President's personal representative, should have the final authority below Presidential level.

This organizational construct then enables each reconstruction team, from village or neighborhood to national levels, to have an arbi-

---

[4] For the command structure in Vietnam, see Dunn (1972, pp. 14–15). For a discussion of the bureaucratic debate and conflict that led to this command structure, see Long (forthcoming).

ter above it if it is unable to reach a consensus decision on actions. Decisionmaking is thus highly decentralized while enhancing unity of effort across all elements of U.S. national power. This structure would essentially replace or override all existing organizational constructs, a radical organizational change. Currently, PRTs are something of a sideshow.[5] Instead, they should be the basis for COIN similar to the Malaya model, with the ambassador atop the whole organizational pyramid for both the military and civilian agencies, as in Figure 6.2.

Further, special attention should be given to coordinating intelligence from all sources at each organizational level. The name "Phoenix" has became a contentious one after Vietnam, yet it is this type of intelligence coordination targeted at the underpinnings of insurgent organizations that is needed.[6] Again, the intelligence community, accustomed to compartmentalization, may balk at this, but it is vital to the COIN effort. In the Phoenix program, intelligence was coordinated at the district and provincial levels with an eye toward targeting the insurgent infrastructure. This organization should be a model for current efforts, with an intelligence center reporting to each level of reconstruction team.

This organization is not a recipe for COIN utopia. The Village Intelligence Center will most likely be an overworked police officer or two working with an equally overworked U.S. noncommissioned officer (NCO), with occasional input from a USAID development manager. Nonetheless, it is an improvement on the current system (or lack thereof).

In addition to changes to the overall organization of COIN, some additional changes must be undertaken by the military. The U.S. military must be further weaned from thinking in terms of divisions and brigades for COIN. Its willingness to task organized smaller units and the recent move toward Unit of Action formations are encouraging, but are not enough. Separate brigades are not bad, but are insufficient

---

[5]   In Afghanistan, PRTs accounted for only about $100 million out of $1.4 billion non–security-related funds obligated in 2004. See Serchuk (2005).

[6]   See Moyar (1997) for a somewhat revisionist overview of Phoenix.

for COIN, as the Soviets found in Afghanistan.[7] COIN is fought at the neighborhood and village level, and is ultimately won or lost by sergeants, lieutenants, and captains, not by colonels and generals. The current focus on force protection combined with a propensity for thinking in terms of high-intensity combat has meant that there is often less autonomy for these squad, platoon, and company leaders than successful COIN requires.

Figure 6.2
Notional Organization for COIN

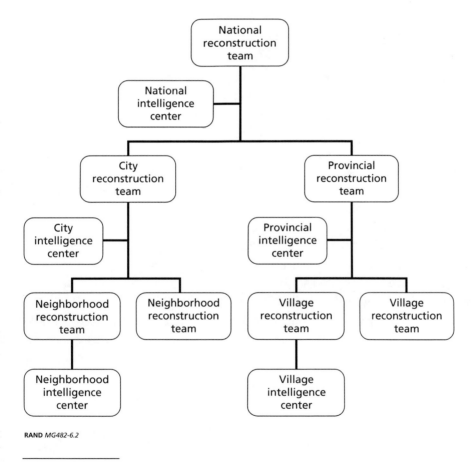

RAND *MG482-6.2*

---

[7] The Soviets created two separate Motorized Rifle Brigades, with a structure not entirely different from a U.S. Armored Cavalry Regiment. See Grau (1996, pp. 80, 101).

Related to this is the potential need for these small units to act as cadres for indigenous forces. This is already being done to some extent by advisers in Iraq, but this appears to be generally at the battalion level. What may be needed hearkens back to the CAP and Civilian Irregular Defense Group (CIDG) programs in Vietnam, where a squad or platoon is embedded for an extended period in an indigenous platoon or company. This provides confidence and training to the nascent indigenous force as well as a secure lifeline to U.S. indirect fire assets.

Some might argue, as in Vietnam, that there are insufficient troops to use *encadrement*. Yet it actually empowers, as it makes effective indigenous units that would otherwise be ineffective. If a six-person U.S. squad makes an 18-person indigenous platoon combat-effective (even if not as proficient as a U.S. platoon), then personnel are essentially tripled. It is true that it may not be possible to *encadre* all indigenous units simultaneously. However, this does not render the idea without merit, as even limited *encadrement* would be an improvement.

Finally, effective metrics for COIN must be established. While far more easily said than done, previous efforts like HES can at least provide a starting point for current efforts. The recent discussion among officers in the Army and the intelligence community about the importance of "atmospherics," such as the number of children seen playing in the street, indicate that at least some are already moving in this direction. The *National Strategy for Victory in Iraq* encouragingly provides a list of metrics as well. These include such things as voter registration and turnout, quantity and quality of Iraqi security forces, and per capita gross domestic product (GDP) (NSC, 2005, pp. 12–13).

While these metrics may be useful, more are needed, particularly at the lower levels that are currently dominated by "atmosphererics." The difficulty in metrics for COIN is striking a balance between the need for standardization of metrics and the need for nuance and detail. Without standardization, metrics are highly subjective and difficult to compare across regions. Without detail and nuance, aggregate measures tell very little about a conflict. In Vietnam, HES, while never perfect, was intended to strike this balance by providing a standard template for metrics at the lowest level of political organization—the hamlet. A similar template is needed for COIN today.

One important addition to this is the vital importance of "blue force" analysis in COIN. It is often difficult for military commanders to assess their efforts objectively without a readily accessible external metric, such as the distance advanced toward an objective. As metrics are being developed, care should be taken to ensure that they assess the actions and performance of blue forces as accurately as possible. For example, the effects of convoy and patrol size, time of travel, speed of travel, route, and the like should be monitored and plotted against insurgent attacks (via IED as well as direct and indirect fire). Some efforts to do this are under way, but more needs to be done.

Open Arms, Open Wallets: Amnesty and Reward

The second major recommendation concerns amnesty and reward, as well as the general problem of enemy motivation and morale. In both Iraq and Afghanistan, amnesty programs, possibly modeled on the late stages of Chieu Hoi, should be implemented. The amnesty should be conditioned on full cooperation with the government, but otherwise should be open to all applicants, even those who have killed Iraqis, Americans, or other nationals in the course of the insurgency. Those who participate should be assisted in relocating with their families away from insurgent-dominated areas in order to prevent insurgent reprisal.

This will be a hard sell in Iraq, where the Shi'a-dominated government is resistant to amnesty for killers of civilians and the U.S. military is equally reluctant to grant amnesty to those who have killed Americans. Conversely, some limited amnesty has been offered in Afghanistan already, providing a starting point for expansion. However, in both countries, a "fight to the finish" with insurgents who might otherwise be convinced or coerced into quitting would be counterproductive.

Further, the possible use of significant rewards as part of this program should be investigated, not just for senior leaders such as Saddam Hussein or Abu Musab al-Zarqawi, but also for rank-and-file members of the insurgency. As in Malaya, information leading to the capture or killing of any insurgents should be well-rewarded. Even if rewards equivalent to those offered in Malaya (in 2005 dollars) were offered and accepted, the entire program would be quite inexpensive by the standards of current expenditures in Iraq. Assuming an average reward of $10,000 per insurgent and a total number of insurgents and active supporters of 50,000, the program would cost only $500 million to "buy off" the entire rank and file of the insurgency. While this outcome is highly unlikely, it iterates the point made in RAND's earlier research: Amnesty and reward can be extremely cost-effective. The current program for rewarding tips in Iraq is woefully underfunded, with a spending rate of less than $5,000 per month.[8] Figure 6.3 shows reward photos used in one such program.

This should also be extended to IED and weapon buy-backs, which are currently conducted on an ad hoc and poorly funded basis. While there is currently no shortage of weapons in Iraq and Afghanistan, the domestic supply is not infinite. Combined with efforts to control the borders, the laws of supply and demand will drive prices up, and the United States should easily be able to outbid even well-financed insurgents.

Amnesty and reward come with caveats. (As the reader will have noted, all recommendations come with caveats.) First, responsiveness to amnesty and reward has much to do with success in other aspects of COIN, especially the provision of security. However, by creating an attractive exit option for insurgents, U.S. COIN forces will not, in effect, be faced with the "cornered rat" problem. Insurgents who might otherwise fight on when hard-pressed because they believe they have no other option could be induced out of the movement rather than having to be killed. Each defector or informer brings valuable intelligence while weakening the morale and confidence of those who continue to fight.

Rewards also create possible moral-hazard problems. If COIN forces lack information, citizens could potentially inform on noninsurgents who are their enemies for purely domestic reasons. So if one feels wronged by a fellow citizen, why not denounce the wrongdoer as an insurgent, thereby getting the wrongdoer arrested and getting paid

---

[8] This section, and particularly data on current COIN, draws heavily on Jackson and Long (2005).

Figure 6.3
The Rewards for Justice Program Currently Focuses Only on High-Level
Terrorists and Insurgents Such as the Late Abu Musab Al-Zarqawi

SOURCE: RewardsForJustice.net.

RAND MG482-6.3

as well?[9] This problem is real, but can be reduced by requiring multiple source confirmation before arrest as well as by validating the accuracy of information after arrest but before the reward is paid.

In addition, any amnesty program raises the problem of morality versus expediency. As was the case with the recent amnesty for the paramilitary Autodefensas Unidas de Colombia (United Self-Defense of Colombia, or AUC), many people will be offended at letting murderers go unpunished. This is also a serious problem, but this author favors expediency in the name of future national unity to justice for individuals.

Similarly, insurgents will need some credible assurance that they will not be treated badly if they surrender. Abu Ghraib and the current stories of torture by the Iraqi Ministry of the Interior have done much

---

[9] For theoretical and empirical discussion of this problem, see Kalyvas (2006).

to reduce the credibility of these potential assurances (see Knickmeyer, 2005). While this damage may not be irrevocable, these practices must be countered by a combination of information operations and the creation of safe, relatively transparent amnesty centers modeled on those of the Chieu Hoi program.

Finally, a new Motivation and Morale study is needed. The motivations of insurgents in Iraq and Afghanistan appear to be at least as multifaceted as those of insurgents in Vietnam. While something appears to be known about the general categories of insurgents (jihadists, Ba'athist remnants, Sunni "rejectionists"), little is known about micro-incentives that motivate individuals to join. For example, are those who emplace IEDs in Iraq primarily motivated by a desire to harm coalition forces, or are they more motivated by insurgent incentives (cash payments to the unemployed) and disincentives (threats to harm family or friends)? What is the actual role of Islamist ideology in motivating the rank and file of insurgents (as opposed to the cadre)?[10]

Further, the overall knowledge of why people fight has not advanced significantly since World War II. A recent Army War College study on morale of both U.S. and Iraqi troops in 2003 prominently cites two studies from World War II, yet both of these older studies have significant methodological problems with their conclusions.[11] A new Motivation and Morale study could potentially advance both the specific knowledge of insurgents in current COIN and add to the overall understanding of the elusive but vital concept of morale.

This new Motivation and Morale study should be kept apart from interrogation for tactical and operational intelligence. Instead, it should rely on participants in the amnesty program as well as on interviews (not interrogations) conducted with captured insurgents. It need not be conducted by RAND (or any other contractor for that

---

[10] Within most if not all revolutions, there appears to be a disconnect between the ideology as interpreted by the elite cadre and the rank-and-file members. See Scott (1979).

[11] Wong (2003). The two studies cited are Marshall (1947) and Shils and Janowitz (1948). For a critique of Marshall, see Glenn (2000). For a critique of Shils and Janowitz, see Bartov (1991).

matter). However, it will require the dedication of a sizable number of individuals to formulate and apply a questionnaire and then compile and analyze the results.

The Khalilzad Lines? Border Security in Iraq and Afghanistan

The third major recommendation[12] is that major border security systems should be seriously investigated for both Iraq and Afghanistan. In Iraq, the cross-border infiltration of personnel, and particularly materiel, is a significant (though admittedly not well-quantified) problem. The western part of Iraq along the Syrian and Jordanian borders appears to be particularly troublesome. Similarly, the border region of Afghanistan and Pakistan appears to be highly unstable, with insurgents able to find shelter in western Pakistan's tribal regions.[13]

In both cases, a security system could attenuate infiltration significantly. The terrain of Afghanistan is problematic for such efforts, but the terrain also makes border crossing more difficult. Conversely, the border in Iraq is easily traversed, but is also relatively easily barricaded. Such border security systems are potentially expensive, but provide an excellent point of leverage for U.S. advantages in technology and capital. The French were able to halt infiltration in terrain somewhat similar to Iraq's almost five decades ago; the United States could do far better now.

For example, remote-piloted vehicles (RPVs) cued by ground-based seismic sensors along the Iraq-Syria-Jordan border could cost-

---

[12] The title of this section only reflects Ambassador Khalilzad's key leadership in both Iraq and Afghanistan and should not be interpreted as an endorsement of these concepts by him.

[13] For a lengthy argument on the utility of border security in current COIN, see Staniland (2005–2006). Staniland also points out the somewhat limited utility of cross-border operations, which, according to one recent report, the U.S. military is already conducting in Syria. See Hersh (2005). One exception to the limited effectiveness of cross-border operations in COIN was the British "Claret" series of operations during the Indonesian *Konfrontasi*. See Mockaitis (1995, pp. 32–39).

effectively monitor infiltration. Combined with multiple fence lines to delay crossing, infiltrators could rapidly be identified and interdicted, either with fires or by mobile pursuit forces. The highly mobile Third Armored Cavalry Regiment, currently attempting to interdict insurgents in western Iraq without the aid of a border security system, would be an ideal pursuit force and would benefit greatly from cuing provided by the system.[14] Iraqi Interior Ministry forces that would also staff checkpoints at legitimate border crossings would supplement these mobile pursuit forces.

As noted earlier, most of the personnel power of the Iraqi insurgency appears to be domestic rather than foreign. This leads some to question the need for border security, if it will only deprive the insurgency of a small portion of its personnel. While a valid concern, there are reasons that argue for controlling the border. First, given the billions being spent on Iraq monthly, a border security system that eliminated only 5 percent of insurgent personnel at a price of less than a billion dollars would still be cost-effective. The relatively uncluttered border region is also a much better place for the United States to employ sensors than are the crowded streets of cities. Anyone attempting to cut through multiple fences along the border is readily classifiable as an insurgent in a way that is impossible to attain in the interior.

In addition, some terrorism analysts are concerned that fighters well-trained and experienced in Iraq will go abroad to cause future troubles. Border control would work both ways, preventing terrorists from leaving Iraq as well. Finally, and perhaps most importantly, much more than personnel power flows across the porous Iraqi border. Money, smuggled goods including oil, and munitions expertise are among the many critical supporting elements of the insurgency that flow into and out of Iraq.

The case for a border security system in Afghanistan is even clearer. Taliban remnants, supported by ethnic Pashtuns and bolstered by a mix of other skilled foreign fighters, use Pakistan's semilawless Northwest Frontier region as a sanctuary. Pakistani intelligence sup-

---

[14] See Finer (2005) for comments on Third Armored Cavalry Regiment (ACR) operations. Marines are also conducting operations along the Syrian border; see Anderson (2005).

ported the Taliban in the 1990s, and some elements may continue to do so or at least turn a blind eye. Rather than a continuous system as in Iraq, this system would probably seek to monitor and control major access routes along the border. Even if only moderately effective, the system would do much to deny insurgent ability to attack in Afghanistan and then retreat to safety across the border.

Some care should go into planning these systems, as the potential for unintended consequences is not insignificant. For example, many inhabitants of the Iraqi border region have lived by smuggling for years, sometimes generations. Depriving them of their livelihood, even in the name of a democratic Iraq, is unlikely to gain their loyalty. Plans would have to be generated to compensate and retrain these citizens. However, there are also potential positive consequences apart from reducing infiltration. One ready example of this is that building and maintaining a border security system will require significant amounts of local labor, people who might otherwise be unemployed.

An End to Streets Without Joy: Security, Development, and Pacification

The fourth and last set of recommendations has to do with the general concept of pacification. Acknowledging that development and area security are inseparable is a key first step, and area security is more than occasional patrols from a secure camp or fortified post.[15] Instead, a permanent security presence must be established, either along the lines of the French system of *quadrillage* in Algeria or the paramilitary Popular Forces in Vietnam, probably combined with some *encadrement* by U.S. forces. These paramilitary forces constitute a bridge between police and the military in terms of capability, and support the functioning of both.

---

[15] This approach was common in Vietnam and appears to be a common feature of regular armies engaging irregular opponents. For a brief discussion of the problems of this approach, see Hoffman (1984).

The formation of militias for local security is already happening de facto in much of Iraq. The former insurgents of the Kurdish *pesh merga* have never disbanded; they have been joined by a variety of Shi'a militias, including the Badr Brigade and the Mahdi Army. This de facto effort needs to be co-opted or preempted where possible. This has been difficult, but a national program along the lines of the later period of the Regional/Popular Forces might be able to incorporate at least some of these militias into the government. Again, the United States should be able to outbid most militias, at least in terms of monetary payments. This provides a major incentive for the poor who might otherwise have no stake to join. *Encadrement* with U.S. or coalition forces would provide reassurance, training, and, critically, monitoring of these local forces to ensure that they do not simply function as "death squads."

In addition to security, development should be primarily local and selective. Areas that are cooperative in terms of providing information on insurgents and being willing to organize in their own defense should be rewarded with additional development funds. The source of these funds should be something like the Malayan RIDA, an entity solely concerned with local rather than national economic development. These should be complemented and supplemented by the efforts of the various levels of reconstruction teams. As noted, national development should not be ignored, particularly in terms of infrastructure, but local development should be the priority. This recommendation is consonant with strategic pillars four and five of the *National Strategy for Victory in Iraq*, but has more local focus (NSC, 2005, pp. 31–32).

Finally, and perhaps most importantly, a census and national identification card system should be created in both Iraq and Afghanistan. Further, a permanent office for creating and developing such systems in less-developed countries should be established (probably in USAID).[16] The idea of effective population control without actually knowing the population is questionable at best. The identification card should obvi-

---

[16] USAID already conducts some work of this sort, but a permanent office devoted it to would both improve the institutional standing of identification and census systems and create a permanent home for "lessons learned" about the problems of implementing these systems in violent or undeveloped regions.

ously be hard to counterfeit or tamper with, and could be tied to the provision of subsidized goods, such as food. It would also be worthwhile to consider implementing something like the Census Grievance program in Vietnam, where the task of census taking and record keeping is combined with an intelligence-gathering function.

Conclusion: Back to the Future?

Regardless of whether one accepts or rejects these suggestions, one key point is all but indisputable. The United States, by virtue of its massive nuclear and conventional capability, has driven almost all potential opponents to embrace terrorism and insurgency as their only potentially viable theory of victory. Preparing for the challenge of COIN can no longer be allowed to wax and wane as it did during the Cold War. Instead, the United States must seriously study what lessons can be gleaned from the study of COIN past as it develops the forces, training, and doctrine for the inevitable COIN of the future.

RAND Counterinsurgency Publications, 1955–1995: Selected Annotated Bibliography

This bibliography is far from exhaustive, and is intended to highlight RAND works that are either of very high salience to current conflicts or are not well-known due to their age, or both. Some of the documents cited herein were part of RAND's D series of publications, which were intended to promote discussion among researchers. Those publications were not reviewed and were never intended for external dissemination, yet provide interesting insights into the debate with RAND on these issues at the time. Not all D-series publications are available to the public. Additionally, note that RAND is continually making documents available; as this book went to press, more of the documents cited were being added. Therefore, the absence of a URL in an entry does not necessarily indicate that it is unavailable now.

Anderson, Mary E., Michael E. Arnsten, and Harvey A. Averch, *Insurgent Organization and Operations: A Case Study of the Viet Cong in the Delta*, 1964–1966, RM-5239-1-ISA/ARPA, 1967. Online at http://www.rand.org/pubs/research_memoranda/RM5239-1/ (as of February 15, 2006.) A detailed examination of insurgent organization and operations in the Mekong Delta province of Dinh Tuong. Describes the interrelation of the political, military, and support infrastructure elements of insurgent organization. Also provides analysis of insurgent defensive, offensive, and logistic operations. A very fine-grained analysis, including appendixes on the history and organization of three specific insurgent battalions, as well as insurgent military intelligence, communication, and training.

Benoit, C., *Conversations with Rural Vietnamese*, D-20138-ARPA/AGILE, 1970. A report based on the author's unstructured conversations with over 100 rural Vietnamese, both peasant and government personnel, as well as discussions with U.S. personnel. Provides a good template for how understanding pacification is actually achieved in other than theoretical or quantitative fashion.

Blaufarb, Douglas S., *Organizing and Managing Unconventional War in Laos, 1962–1970*, R-919-ARPA, 1972. Author is the former Chief of Station for the CIA in Laos and the analysis is based on his personal experience. Illustrates many of the factors that made counterinsurgency in Laos unique, particularly the Geneva Accords, which were supposed to yield a neutral Laos and the separate interdiction effort run from Vietnam against the Ho Chi Minh. Argues strongly for the importance of a single-manager approach to counterinsurgency, in this case the U.S. Ambassador.

Carrier, J. M., and Charles Alexander Holmes Thomson, *Viet Cong Motivation and Morale: The Special Case of Chieu Hoi*, RM-4830-2-ISA/ARPA, 1966. Online at http://www.rand.org/pubs/research_memoranda/RM4830-2 (as of July 7, 2006). Presents the results of RAND analysis of interviews conducted with participants (known as "ralliers") in the South Vietnamese amnesty program known as Chieu Hoi ("Open Arms"). Conclusions include the importance of propaganda reassuring potential ralliers that they will receive equitable treatment and that individual rather than ideological motivations dominate the decision to rally. Ralliers should also be incorporated into the propaganda effort, and particular attention should be paid to propaganda directed at the families of potential ralliers.

Carter, Gregory A., and M. B. Schaffer, *On Some Counterproductive Aspects of Tactical Force Employment in South Vietnam: Interviews with Vietnamese Prisoners and Civilians*, D-16278-PR, 1967. Analyzes a sample of RAND interviews with insurgent prisoners and South Vietnamese civilians to determine the negative impact of civilian death and destruction caused by indirect fire on the broader counterinsurgency effort. The assessment, crosschecked with a CBS poll of South Vietnamese civilians, is that the average civilian appears at least as likely to blame the insurgents as the counterinsurgents for such collateral damage. This challenges the conventional wisdom that such efforts are inherently counterproductive.

Cochran, S. W., *Some Questions—Some Answers*, D-16157-ISA/ARPA, 1967. Draws together into a short set of questions and answers many of the findings of the Viet Cong Motivation and Morale study. Includes an annotated bibliography.

Donnell, J. C., *Viet Cong Recruitment: Why and How Men Join*, D-14436-ISA/ARPA, 1966. Lengthy treatment of VC recruitment as part of the Motivation and Morale Study. Documents the shift from careful, voluntary recruitment to a more coercive form of recruitment. Highlights the variety of motivations for joining.

Elliott, David W. P., and W. A. Stewart, *Pacification and the Viet Cong System in Dinh Tuong: 1966–1967*, RM-5788-ISA/ARPA, 1969. Online at http://www.rand.org/pubs/research_memoranda/RM5788/ (as of July 7, 2006). Analyzes the response of the Viet Cong "system" (consisting of political and military elements) in one province to U.S.-GVN pacification efforts. The authors argue that the system is incredibly strong due to the reinforcing elements of the system but potentially vulnerable to disruption as it is cumbersome and bureaucratic.

Ellis, John Winthrop, and M. B. Schaffer, *Three Months in Vietnam—A Trip Report: The Paramilitary War*, D-16004-PR, 1967. Edited transcript of a briefing on a trip to Vietnam. Focus is on the paramilitary side of the war. Comes to some thoughtful conclusions about the inability to reverse some of the effects of insurgency and counterinsurgency in less than a generation.

Ellsberg, Daniel, *Revolutionary Judo: Working Notes on Vietnam No. 10*, D-19807-ARPA/AGILE, 1970. A counterpoint to Leites and Wolf's *Rebellion and Authority* (1970), using the same language. Argues that preferences of the population matter because they change the average and marginal costs of extracting resources from the population for both the government and insurgents. Further, insurgents are often able to provoke the government into responses that make the population more sympathetic to the insurgents, essentially using the greater strength of the government against itself.

Farmer, J. A., *Counterinsurgency: Principles and Practices in Viet-Nam*, P-3039, 1964. Online at http://www.rand.org/pubs/papers/P3039 (as of July 6, 2006). Edited transcript of a briefing given on counterinsurgency at the Naval Reserve Officers School. Presents a brief overview of counterinsurgency, with an interesting section on indicators in counterinsurgency.

Galula, David, *Pacification in Algeria, 1956-1958*, RM-3878-ARPA, 1963. Galula served in French COIN efforts in Algeria after spending time as an attaché in Hong Kong observing COIN in East Asia. His observations on his experiences, published as *Counterinsurgency Warfare: Theory and Practice* (1964), have made him one of the central figures of modern COIN writing. Much of his thinking on his experience was initially done at RAND and this lengthy monograph is the result. Republished in 2006 as MG-478-RC, online at http://www.rand.org/pubs/monographs/MG478/ (as of February 15, 2006).

Gouré, Leon, *Inducements and Deterrents to Defection: An Analysis of the Motives of 125 Defectors*, RM-5522-1-ISA/ARPA, 1968. Online at http://www.rand.org/pubs/research_memoranda/RM5522-1/ (as of July 7, 2006). Analysis of motives of defectors from the Viet Cong guerrilla and civilian support infrastructure. Concludes that fear of mistreatment by the government was a major deterrent, as was fear of reprisal against family members in insurgent-controlled areas.

Gouré, Leon, A. J. Russo, and D. Scott, *Some Findings of the Viet Cong Motivation and Morale Study: June–December 1965*, RM-4911-2-ISA/ARPA, 1966. Online at http://www.rand.org/pubs/research_memoranda/RM4911-2/ (as of July 7, 2006). Presents a RAND assessment of interviews with captured and defector insurgents. A central finding is the lack of understanding by most of the populace as to why the United States is involved in Vietnam. Recommendations include increasing propaganda to correct this failing as well as tailoring military efforts to avoid alienating the rural populace.

Heymann, Hans, *Seminar on Development and Security in Thailand: Part I, The Insurgency*, RM-5871-AID/ARPA, 1969. Online at http://www.rand.org/pubs/research_memoranda/RM5871/ (as of July 7, 2006). Presents a view of the sources and methods of the Communist insurgency in Thailand. Discusses, among other things, recruiting techniques and unique conditions of Thailand.

Hickey, Gerald Cannon, *U.S. Strategy in South Vietnam: Extrication and Equilibrium*, D-19736-ARPA, 1969. Examines the status quo in South Vietnam in 1969 and the forces affecting its future equilibrium. Notes that Americans in Vietnam have missed the point that the insurgency is not merely a military conflict, or even a political-military conflict. Instead it is revolutionary, with implications for the society, economy, military, and politics. Discusses these factors in the context of U.S. withdrawal.

Hoffman, Bruce, and Jennifer Taw, *Defense Policy and Low-Intensity Conflict: The Development of Britain's "Small Wars" Doctrine During the 1950s*, R-4015-A, 1991. Similar in tone to the Rhodesia report (Hoffman, Taw, and Arnold, 1991). Focuses on Kenya, Malaya, and Cyprus. Britain was highly constrained in terms of resources but was reasonably effective in developing doctrine for COIN, particularly in terms of appointing a single manager for all COIN operations and focusing on intelligence.

Hoffman, Bruce, Jennifer Taw, and David W. Arnold, *Lessons for Contemporary Counterinsurgencies: The Rhodesian Experience*, R-3998-A, 1991. Specifically written to encourage the U.S. Army to give greater thought to counterinsurgency doctrine. Focuses on the problems of organization for counterinsurgency, pacification, urban terrorism, and intelligence.

Hosmer, Stephen T., *The Army's Role in Counterinsurgency and Insurgency*, R-3947-A, 1990. Online at http://www.rand.org/pubs/reports/R3947/ (as of February 13, 2006). Accurate assessment of the challenges faced by the U.S. Army in counterinsurgency. Argues that the Army should develop a dedicated cadre of COIN experts, and help create a joint COIN training institute. Only dated by the then-current belief in reluctance to commit actual U.S. combat forces to counterinsurgency.

Hosmer, Stephen T., and S. O. Crane, *Counterinsurgency: A Symposium, April 16–20, 1962*, R-412-ARPA, 1963. Online at http://www.rand.org/pubs/reports/R412-1 (as of July 6, 2006). This symposium gathered together several of the most accomplished practitioners of counterinsurgency at the time in an attempt to compare their experiences and derive lessons. An excellent work with continuing relevance, its only weakness is that the question-and-answer and open-ended discussion format can be difficult for the reader to engage.

Jenkins, Brian Michael, *Why the North Vietnamese Keep Fighting*, D-20153-ARPA/AGILE, 1970. Very specific to the late Vietnam-era leadership of North Vietnam, rather than the individual soldier. Does make some useful points, particularly on why attrition-based approaches to warfighting, particularly in limited war or counterinsurgency, are not productive.

Kellen, Konrad, *Conversations with NVA and VC Soldiers: A Study of Enemy Motivation and Morale*, D-18967-ISA, 1969. Kellen, a former interrogator of German prisoners of war (POWs) in World War II, was integral to the RAND Motivation and Morale study. This study attempts to track North Vietnamese Army (NVA) and VC morale several years after the initial Motivation and Morale interviews. The conclusion at which Kellen arrives is that enemy morale in 1969 was at least as high as that in 1965. He argues that the enemy's ability to maintain morale is the main reason for the frustration of American COIN efforts in Vietnam.

Koch, J. A., *The Chieu Hoi Program in South Vietnam, 1963–1971*, R-1172-ARPA, 1973. Comprehensive analysis of the Chieu Hoi amnesty program by a former participant. Provides discussion of the strengths and weaknesses of the program and how it was managed. Particularly notes the cost-effectiveness of the amnesty program.

Komer, Robert W., *Organization and Management of the New Model Pacification Program—1966–1969*, D-20104-ARPA, 1970. Candid discussion of pacification (with additional written amplification by Komer) between Ambassador Komer, the first DEPCORDS in Vietnam; Col. Robert Montague, his primary assistant; and two military historians. Makes several useful observations on pacification, the most important of which are that effective organization for the implementation of known ideas on pacification is more important than new ideas, and that the effect of several average programs that have been coordinated is better for wartime pacification than is seeking to optimize individual programs.

———, *Bureaucracy Does Its Thing: Institutional Constraints on U.S.–GVN Performance in Vietnam*, R-967-ARPA, 1972. An analysis of the limits of bureaucratic adaptation to new challenges. Komer argues that the lack of coordination between bureaucracies in Vietnam was the result of attempting to use institutions in novel ways without creating a new system to coordinate and manage them. This failure led to some deleterious effects, such as fragmentation of effort and overmilitarization.

Leites, Nathan Constantin, and Charles Wolf, Jr., *Rebellion and Authority: An Analytic Essay on Insurgent Conflicts*, R-0462-ARPA, 1970. Online at http://www.rand.org/pubs/reports/R0462/ (as of February 14, 2006). The definitive statement of cost/benefit theory in COIN. Leites and Wolf persuasively argue that insurgency and counterinsurgency should be viewed as opposing systems. The system that is more successful in obtaining inputs (e.g., people, taxation) at a reasonable cost and then converting them into outputs (e.g., soldiers, public good) will triumph.

Maullin, Richard L., *Soldiers, Guerrillas, and Politics in Colombia*, R-0630-ARPA, 1971. Online at http://www.rand.org/pubs/reports/R0630/ (as of February 16, 2006). An assessment of the impact of prolonged insurgency and counterinsurgency operations on a professional military. Suggests that professionalism in the military, far from making it nonpartisan, drives militaries toward political intervention in response to the problems of counterinsurgency. Also provides analysis of the particular responses of the Colombian military.

Melnik, C., *Insurgency and Counterinsurgency in Algeria*, D-10671-1-ISA, 1964. Melnik, an adviser to the French Cabinet, was essentially in charge of police and special services from 1959 to 1962. He provides a candid assessment of both the facts of the Algerian war and the theoretical under-pinnings of insurgency and counterinsurgency. Many of his arguments prefigure those elaborated in other RAND writings, such as Ellsberg's *Revolutionary Judo* (1970). Also notes the nonuniform character of the FLN, particularly in its early stages.

Pauker, Guy J., *Notes on Non-Military Measures in Control of Insurgency*, P-2642, 1962. Online at http://www.rand.org/pubs/papers/P2642 (as of July 6, 2006). Brief assessment of the nonmilitary factors contributing to successful counterinsurgency in the Philippines and Malaya during the late 1940s through the 1950s. Concludes that control of the population and the successful reassertion of government authority are central. Social revolution is viewed as less important than restoring the confidence of the population in government.

———, *Government Responses to Armed Insurgency in Southeast Asia: A Comparative Examination of Failures and Successes and Their Likely Implications for the Future*, P-7081, 1985. Online at http://www.rand.org/pubs/papers/P7081/ (as of February 14, 2006). A brief comparison of COIN techniques and their results in Indonesia, Thailand, Malaysia, the Philippines, and Burma. Concludes that COIN efforts that do not incorporate serious political-economic efforts, co-equal with military efforts, are destined to result in stalemate at best.

Paxson, Edwin W., *The Sierra Project—A Study of Limited Wars: Presented to the Air Staff in Washington*, B-41, 1958. An early simulation study of limited wars. Focuses on semiconventional conflict similar to the late stages of the Viet Minh war against the French in Indochina rather than counterinsurgency.

Pye, Lucian W., *Observations on the Chieu Hoi Program*, RM-4864-1-ISA/ ARPA, 1966. This brief analytic note argues that Chieu Hoi is under-utilized and undersupported by both the U.S. and South Vietnamese governments. Calls for a reconceptualization of Chieu Hoi as a program for national development and unification. The program should distinguish between refugees, marginal insurgent defectors, active insurgent defectors, and prisoners. Clear incentives tailored to each group should be articulated and scrupulously adhered to. Further, much greater effort to incorporate highly talented insurgent defectors into propaganda and counterinsurgency should be undertaken.

Schwarz, Benjamin, *American Counterinsurgency Doctrine and El Salvador: The Frustrations of Reform and the Illusions of Nation Building*, R-4042-USDP, 1991. Online at http://www.rand.org/pubs/reports/R4042/ (as of February 13, 2006). A very negative assessment of U.S. counterinsurgency in El Salvador. Focuses on the inability of the U.S government to obtain sufficient leverage over the government of El Salvador to force it to institute real political, economic, or military reform. Rightly points to numerous failures, but ignores the not insignificant (if uneven) progress on reform made during the course of the war by the government of El Salvador. Ironically, a durable ceasefire was signed between the government and the insurgents only a few months after the publication of this report. This outcome does not obviate many of his points on the difficulty of COIN, as the end of the conflict stemmed in large part from the end of the Cold War.

Sweetland, A., *Item Analysis of the HES (Hamlet Evaluation System)*, D-17634-ARPA/AGILE, 1968. Assesses the components of the HES used in South Vietnam. By attempting to determine which components correlate little with one another but strongly with the total HES score, the components that seem to account most strongly for successful pacification can be isolated. The components related to security and development, intuitively and theoretically appealing, do appear to account for most of the variance. Suggestions for improving the HES, such as weighting some components more than others and adding some additional components (such as hamlet taxation by insurgents) are made.

Weiner, Milton G., and Marvin Schaffer, *Border Security in South Vietnam*, R-0572-ARPA, 1971. Online at http://www.rand.org/pubs/reports/R0572/ (as of February 15, 2006). Provides a comprehensive assessment of providing border security in South Vietnam. Compares the costs and benefits of three systems (enhanced surveillance; surveillance plus strong points; and surveillance, strong points, and a continuous barrier) when applied to three models of infiltration (small groups, large guerrilla groups, and large regular units). Concludes that the staffed strongpoint system was most cost-effective.

Wohlstetter, Albert, *Comments on the Wolf-Leites Manuscript: "Rebellion and Authority,"* D(L)-17701-ARPA/AGILE, 1968. Online at http://www. rand.org/publications/classics/wohlstetter/DL17701/DL17701.html (as of February 13, 2006). Available online, but probably overlooked. Offers thoughtful comments on preferences in cost/benefit analysis of insurgency. Makes the point that preference distribution among the population can potentially have major consequences in terms of "tipping points" for insurgency (compare to Petersen, 2001).

Wolf, Charles, Jr., *Insurgency and Counterinsurgency: New Myths and Old Realities*, P-3132-1, 1965. Online at http://www.rand.org/pubs/papers/P3132-1/ (as of February 14, 2006). A brief overview of the counterinsurgency paradigm discussed in more detail in *Rebellion and Authority* (Leites and Wolf, 1970). Particularly useful as it makes recommendations on the value of rewards for information and defection, the virtue of amnesty programs, the possibilities of food control, and the possible paradox of development actually increasing insurgent capabilities even as it decreases support for insurgents.

Zwick, C. J., Charles A. Cooper, Hans Heymann, and Richard H. Moorsteen. *U.S. Economic Assistance in Vietnam: A Proposed Reorientation*, R-0430-AID, 1964. A somewhat contrarian analysis of development aid in support of counterinsurgency that calls for an expansionary economic policy, but one targeted on the centers of government support, the urban areas, and well-pacified rural areas. Rather than attempting to increase the welfare of the populace as a whole, which could create more resources for insurgents to tax, this targeted program would serve as an incentive for citizens to support pacification. Other, more specific recommendations, such as the elimination of unpaid communal labor, are made as well.

References

Allen, George W., *None So Blind: A Personal Account of the Intelligence Failure in Vietnam*, Chicago: Ivan R. Dee, 2001.

Allen, Thomas B., *War Games: The Secret World of the Creators, Players and Policy Makers Rehearsing World War III Today*, New York: McGraw-Hill, 1987.

Anderson, John Ward, "U.S. Widens Offensive in Far Western Iraq; Insurgent Positions Near Syria Targeted," *The Washington Post*, November 15, 2005, p. A16.

Anderson, Mary E., Michael E. Arnsten, and Harvey A. Averch, *Insurgent Organization and Operations: A Case Study of the Viet Cong in the Delta, 1964–1966*, Santa Monica, Calif.: RAND Corporation, RM-5239-1-ISA/ARPA, 1967. Online at http://www.rand.org/pubs/research_memoranda/RM5239-1/ (as of February 15, 2006).

Aussaresses, Paul, *The Battle of the Casbah: Terrorism and Counter-Terrorism in Algeria, 1955–1957*, Robert L. Miller, trans., New York: Enigma Books, 2002.

Bartov, Omer, *Hitler's Army: Soldiers, Nazis, and War in the Third Reich*, New York: Oxford University Press, 1991.

Baumann, Robert F., *Russian-Soviet Unconventional Wars in the Caucasus, Central Asia, and Afghanistan*, Fort Leavenworth, Kan.: Combat Studies Institute, 1993. Online at http://www.cgsc.army.mil/carl/resources/csi/content.asp#russ (as of February 14, 2006).

Beckett, I. F. W., *Insurgency in Iraq: An Historical Perspective*, Carlisle, Pa.: Strategic Studies Institute, 2005. Online at http://www.strategicstudiesinstitute.army.mil/pdffiles/PUB592.pdf (as of February 14, 2006).

Bennet, James, "The Mystery of the Insurgency," *The New York Times*, May 15, 2005, Sec. 4, p. 4.

Benoit, C., *Conversations with Rural Vietnamese*, Santa Monica, Calif.: RAND Corporation, D-20138-ARPA/AGILE, 1970.

Bigeard, Marcel-Maurice, *Ma Guerre d'Indochine*, Paris: Hachette, 1994.

———, *Ma Guerre d'Algérie*, Paris: Hachette, 1995.

———, *Pour Une Parcelle de Gloire*, Paris: Edition 01, 1997.

Blackmer, Donald L. M., *The MIT Center for International Studies: The Founding Years 1951–1969*, Cambridge, Mass.: MIT Center for International Studies, 2002.

Blaufarb, Douglas S., *Organizing and Managing Unconventional War in Laos, 1962–1970*, Santa Monica, Calif.: RAND Corporation, R-919-ARPA, 1972a.

———, *Organizing Counterinsurgency in Thailand, 1962–1970*, Santa Monica, Calif.: RAND Corporation, 1972b. Not reviewed for public release.

Byman, Daniel, Peter Chalk, Bruce Hoffman, William Rosenau, and David Brannan, *Trends in Outside Support for Insurgent Movements*, Santa Monica, Calif.: RAND Corporation, MR-1405-OTI, 2001. Online at http://www.rand.org/pubs/monograph_reports/MR1405/ (as of February 13, 2006).

Canby, Steven L., Brian Michael Jenkins, and R. B. Rainey, *A Ground Force Structure and Strategy for Vietnam in the 1970's*, Santa Monica, Calif.: RAND Corporation, D-20148-1-ARPA, 1970.

Carrier, J. M., and Charles Alexander Holmes Thomson, *Viet Cong Motivation and Morale: The Special Case of Chieu Hoi*, Santa Monica, Calif.: RAND Corporation, RM-4830-2-ISA/ARPA, 1966. Online at http://www.rand.org/pubs/research_memoranda/RM4830-2/ (as of July 7, 2006).

Carter, Gregory A., and M. B. Schaffer, *On Some Counterproductive Aspects of Tactical Force Employment in South Vietnam: Interviews with Vietnamese Prisoners and Civilians*, Santa Monica, Calif.: RAND Corporation, D-16278-PR, 1967.

Central Intelligence Agency, Directorate of Intelligence, *El Salvador: Guerilla Capabilities and Prospects Over the Next Two Years*, October 1984.

CIA. See Central Intelligence Agency.

Cochran, S. W., *Some Questions—Some Answers*, Santa Monica, Calif.: RAND Corporation, D-16157-ISA/ARPA, 1967.

Coll, Steve, *Ghost Wars: The Secret History of the CIA, Afghanistan, and bin Laden, from the Soviet Invasion to September 10, 2001*, New York: Penguin Press, 2004.

Coll, Steve, and Susan B. Glasser, "Terrorists Turn to the Web as Base of Operations," *The Washington Post*, August 7, 2005, p. A01.

Collins, James Lawton, *The Development and Training of the South Vietnamese Army, 1950–1972*, Washington, D.C.: Department of the Army, 1975. Online at http://purl.access.gpo.gov/GPO/LPS41246 (as of March 17, 2006).

———, *The Development and Training of the South Vietnamese Army, 1950–1972*, Washington, D.C.: Department of the Army, 1991.

Collins, Martin J., *Planning for Modern War: RAND and the Air Force, 1945–1950*, College Park, Md.: University of Maryland, Ph.D. thesis, 1998.

Community Policing Consortium, *Understanding Community Policing: A Framework for Action*, Washington, D.C.: Bureau of Justice Assistance, 1994. Online at http://www.ncjrs.gov/txtfiles/commp.txt (as of February 15, 2006).

Conrad, Joseph, *Heart of Darkness*, Cheswold, Del.: Prestwick House, 2004.

Davison, W. Phillips, *User's Guide to the RAND Interviews in Vietnam*, Santa Monica, Calif.: RAND Corporation, R-1024-ARPA, 1972. Online at http://www.rand.org/pubs/reports/R1024 (as of July 6, 2006).

Digby, Jim, "RAND in the 1950s," in Andrew W. Marshall, J. J. Martin, and Henry S. Rowen, eds., *On Not Confusing Ourselves: Essays on National Security Strategy in Honor of Albert and Roberta Wohlstetter*, Boulder, Colo.: Westview Press, 1991, pp. 17–28.

Donnell, J. C., *Viet Cong Recruitment: Why and How Men Join*, Santa Monica, Calif.: RAND Corporation, D-14436-ISA/ARPA, 1966.

Duiker, William J., *The Communist Road to Power in Vietnam*, 2nd ed., Boulder, Colo.: Westview Press, 1996.

Dunn, Carroll H., *Base Development in South Vietnam 1965–1970*, Washington, D.C.: Department of the Army, 1972.

Elliott, David W. P., and M. Elliott, *Documents of an Elite Viet Cong Delta Unit: The Demolition Platoon of the 514th Battalion—Part 1: Unit Composition and Personnel*, Santa Monica, Calif.: RAND Corporation, RM-5848-ISA/ARPA, 1969a. Online at http://www.rand.org/pubs/research_memoranda/RM5848 (as of July 6, 2006).

——, *Documents of an Elite Viet Cong Delta Unit: The Demolition Platoon of the 514th Battalion—Part Two: Party Organization*, Santa Monica, Calif.: RAND Corporation, RM-5849-ISA/ARPA, 1969b. Online at http://www.rand.org/pubs/research_memoranda/RM5849 (as of July 6, 2006).

——, *Documents of an Elite Viet Cong Delta Unit: The Demolition Platoon of the 514th Battalion—Part Three: Military Organization and Activities*, Santa Monica, Calif.: RAND Corporation, RM-5850-ISA/ARPA, 1969c. Online at http://www.rand.org/pubs/research_memoranda/RM5850 (as of July 6, 2006).

——, *Documents of an Elite Viet Cong Delta Unit: The Demolition Platoon of the 514th Battalion—Part Four: Political Indoctrination and Military Training*, Santa Monica, Calif.: RAND Corporation, RM-5851-ISA-ARPA, 1969d. Online at http://www.rand.org/pubs/research_memoranda/RM5851/ (as of July 6, 2006).

——, *Documents of an Elite Viet Cong Delta Unit: The Demolition Platoon of the 514th Battalion—Part Five: Personal Letters*, Santa Monica, Calif.: RAND Corporation, RM-5852-ISA/ARPA, 1969e. Online at http://www.rand.org/pubs/research_memoranda/RM5852 (as of July 6, 2006).

Elliott, David W. P., and W. A. Stewart, *Pacification and the Viet Cong System in Dinh Tuong: 1966–1967*, Santa Monica, Calif.:

RAND   Corporation,   RM-5788-ISA/ARPA,   1969.   Online   at http://www.rand.org/pubs/research_memoranda/RM5788/ (as of July 7, 2006).

Ellis, John Winthrop, and M. B. Schaffer, *Three Months in Vietnam—A Trip Report: The Paramilitary War*, Santa Monica, Calif.: RAND Corporation, D-16004-PR, 1967.

Ellsberg, Daniel, *Revolutionary Judo: Working Notes on Vietnam No. 10*, Santa Monica, Calif.: RAND Corporation, D-19807-ARPA/AGILE, 1970.

Farmer, J. A., *Counterinsurgency: Principles and Practices in Viet-Nam*, Santa Monica, Calif.: RAND Corporation, P-3039, 1964. Online at http://www.rand.org/pubs/papers/P3039 (as of July 6, 2006).

Finer, Jonathan, "Among Insurgents in Iraq, Few Foreigners Are Found," *The Washington Post*, November 17, 2005, p. A01.

Gaddis, John Lewis, *Strategies of Containment: A Critical Appraisal of Postwar American National Security Policy*, New York: Oxford University Press, 1982.

Gall, Carlotta, "More G.I.'s to Go to Insecure Afghan Areas to Permit Aid Work," *The New York Times*, December 22, 2003, p. A10.

Galula,   David,   *Pacification   in   Algeria,   1956–1958*,   Santa Monica,   Calif.:   RAND   Corporation,   RM-3878-ARPA,   1963. Republished with new foreword as MG-478-RC, 2006; online at http://www.rand.org/pubs/monographs/MG478/ (as of February 15, 2006).

———, *Counterinsurgency Warfare: Theory and Practice*, New York: Praeger, 1964.

———,   *Pacification   in   Algeria,   1956–1958*,   Santa   Monica, Calif.:   RAND   Corporation,   MG-478-RC,   2006.   Online   at http://www.rand.org/pubs/monographs/MG478/ (as of February 15, 2006).

Garamone, Jim, "Discussion Needed to Change Interagency Process, Pace Says," *Armed Forces Information Service News Articles*, September 17, 2004. Online at http://www.defenselink.mil/news/Sep2004/n09172004_2004091704.html (as of February 15, 2006).

Gerwehr, Scott, and Nina Hachigian, "In Iraq's Prisons, Try a Little Tenderness," *The New York Times*, August 25, 2005, p. A23.

Ghamari-Tabrizi, Sharon, *The Worlds of Herman Kahn: The Intuitive Science of Thermonuclear War*, Cambridge, Mass.: Harvard University Press, 2005.

Giap, Vo Nguyen, *People's War, People's Army: The Viet Cong Insurrection Manual for Underdeveloped Countries*, New York: Praeger, 1963.

Glenn, Russell W., *Reading Athena's Dance Card: Men Against Fire in Vietnam*, Annapolis, Md.: Naval Institute Press, 2000.

Gouré, Leon, *Inducements and Deterrents to Defection: An Analysis of the Motives of 125 Defectors*, Santa Monica, Calif.: RAND Corporation, RM-5522-1-ISA/ARPA, 1968. Online at http://www.rand.org/pubs/research_memoranda/RM5522-1/ (as of July 7, 2006).

Gouré, Leon, A. J. Russo, and D. Scott, *Some Findings of the Viet Cong Motivation and Morale Study: June–December 1965*, Santa Monica, Calif.: RAND Corporation, RM-4911-2-ISA/ARPA, 1966. Online at http://www.rand.org/pubs/research_memoranda/RM4911-2/ (as of July 7, 2006).

Gouré, Leon, and C. A. H. Thomson, *Some Impressions of Viet Cong Vulnerabilities: An Interim Report*, Santa Monica, Calif.: RAND Corporation, RM-4699-1-ISA/ARPA, 1965. Online at http://www.rand.org/pubs/research_memoranda/RM4699-1/ (as of July 7, 2006).

Grau, Lester W., *The Bear Went Over the Mountain: Soviet Combat Tactics in Afghanistan*, Washington, D.C.: National Defense University Press, 1996. Online at http://permanent.access.gpo.gov/websites/nduedu/www.ndu.edu/inss/books/Books%20-%201996/Bear%20Went%20Over%20Mountain%20-%20Aug%2096/brormn.pdf (as of February 16, 2006).

Greenwood, Peter W., and Joan R. Petersilia, *The Criminal Investigation Process, Volume I: Summary and Policy Implications*, Santa Monica, Calif.: RAND Corporation, R-1776-DOJ, 1975. Online at http://www.rand.org/pubs/reports/R1776/ (as of February 15, 2006).

Greenwood, Peter W., Jan M. Chaiken, Joan R. Petersilia, Linda L. Prusoff, R. P. Castro, Konrad Kellen, and Sorrel Wildhorn, *The Criminal Investigation Process, Volume III: Observations and Analysis*, Santa Monica, Calif.: RAND Corporation, R-1778-DOJ, 1975. Online at http://www.rand.org/pubs/reports/R1778/ (as of February 15, 2006).

Gurtov, Melvin, *Viet Cong Cadres and the Cadre System: A Study of the Main and Local Forces*, Santa Monica, Calif.: RAND Corporation, 1967. Government publication; not available to the general public.

Gurtov, Melvin, and Konrad Kellen, *Vietnam: Lessons and Mislessons*, Santa Monica, Calif.: RAND Corporation, P-4084, 1969. Online at http://www.rand.org/pubs/papers/P4084/ (as of February 14, 2006).

Hersh, Seymour M., "Annals of National Security: Up in the Air: Bush's Intransigence and the Coming Air War," *The New Yorker*, December 5, 2005, pp. 24–37.

Heymann, Hans, *Seminar on Development and Security in Thailand: Part I, The Insurgency*, Santa Monica, Calif.: RAND Corporation, RM-5871-AID/ARPA, 1969a. Online at http://www.rand.org/pubs/research_memoranda/RM5871/ (as of July 7, 2006).

———, *Seminar on Development and Security in Thailand: Part II, Development-Security Interactions*, Santa Monica, Calif.: RAND Corporation, 1969b. Government publication; not available to the general public.

Hickey, Gerald Cannon, *U.S. Strategy in South Vietnam: Extrication and Equilibrium*, Santa Monica, Calif.: RAND Corporation, D-19736-ARPA, 1969.

Hoffman, Bruce, *The Siege Mentality in Beirut: An Historical Analogy Between the British in Palestine and the Americans in Lebanon*, Santa Monica, Calif.: RAND Corporation, P-6953, 1984. Online at http://www.rand.org/pubs/papers/P6953/ (as of February 13, 2006).

———, *Insurgency and Counterinsurgency in Iraq*, Santa Monica, Calif.: RAND Corporation, OP-127-IPC/CMEPP, 2004. Online at http://www.rand.org/pubs/occasional_papers/OP127/index.html as of February 13, 2006.

Hoffman, Bruce, and Jennifer Taw, *Defense Policy and Low-Intensity Conflict: The Development of Britain's "Small Wars" Doctrine During the 1950s*, Santa Monica, Calif.: RAND Corporation, R-4015-A, 1991. Online at http://www.rand.org/pubs/reports/R4015/ (as of February 13, 2006).

———, *A Strategic Framework for Countering Terrorism and Insurgency*, Santa Monica, Calif.: RAND Corporation, N-3506-DOS, 1992. Online at http://www.rand.org/pubs/notes/N3506/ (as of February 13, 2006).

Hoffman, Bruce, Jennifer Taw, and David W. Arnold, *Lessons for Contemporary Counterinsurgencies: The Rhodesian Experience*, Santa Monica, Calif.: RAND Corporation, R-3998-A, 1991. Online at http://www.rand.org/pubs/reports/R3998/ (as of February 13, 2006).

Horne, Alistair, *A Savage War of Peace: Algeria 1954–1962*, New York: Viking Press, 1978.

———, *A Savage War of Peace: Algeria, 1954–1962*, New York: Penguin Books, 1987.

Hosmer, Stephen, *Viet Cong Repression and Its Implications for the Future*, Santa Monica, Calif.: RAND Corporation, R-0475/1-ARPA, 1970. Online at http://www.rand.org/pubs/reports/R0475.1/ (as of February 13, 2006).

———, *The Army's Role in Counterinsurgency and Insurgency*, Santa Monica, Calif.: RAND Corporation, R-3947-A, 1990. Online at http://www.rand.org/pubs/reports/R3947/ (as of February 13, 2006).

Hosmer, Stephen T., and S. O. Crane, *Counterinsurgency: A Symposium, April 16–20, 1962*, Santa Monica, Calif.: RAND Corporation, R-412-ARPA, 1963. Online at http://www.rand.org/pubs/reports/R412-1 (as of July 6, 2006).

Hosmer, Stephen, Konrad Kellen, and Brian Michael Jenkins, *The Fall of South Vietnam: Statements by Vietnamese Military and Civilian Leaders*, Santa Monica, Calif.: RAND Corporation, R-2208-OSD(HIST), 1978. Online at http://www.rand.org/pubs/reports/R2208/ (as of February 13, 2006).

Hosmer, Stephen, and George K. Tanham, *Countering Covert Aggression*, Santa Monica, Calif.: RAND Corporation, N-2412-USDP, 1986. Online at http://www.rand.org/pubs/notes/N2412/ (as of February 13, 2006).

Huntington, Samuel P., *Political Order in Changing Societies*, New Haven, Conn.: Yale University Press, 1968.

Jackson, Colin, and Austin Long, *Selective Amnesty and Counter-Insurgency: Malaya, Vietnam, and Iraq*, paper presented to the MIT Center for International Studies Insurgency and Irregular Warfare Working Group, October 19, 2005.

Jacoby, Jeff, "Iraq Is No Vietnam," *The Boston Globe*, August 25, 2005, p. A15.

Jenkins, Brian Michael, *The Unchangeable War*, Santa Monica, Calif.: RAND Corporation, RM-6278-2-ARPA, 1970a.

————, *Why the North Vietnamese Keep Fighting*, Santa Monica, Calif.: RAND Corporation, D-20153-ARPA/AGILE, 1970b.

————, *International Terrorism: A New Kind of Warfare*, Santa Monica, Calif.: RAND Corporation, P-5261, 1974. Online at http://www.rand.org/pubs/papers/P5261/ (as of February 13, 2006).

Kalyvas, Stathis N., *The Logic of Violence in Civil War*, Cambridge and New York: Cambridge University Press, 2006.

Kaplan, Fred M., *The Wizards of Armageddon*, Stanford, Calif.: Stanford University Press, 1991.

Kellen, Konrad, *Conversations with NVA and VC Soldiers: A Study of Enemy Motivation and Morale*, Santa Monica, Calif.: RAND Corporation, D-18967-ISA, 1969a.

————, *A View of the VC: Elements of Cohesion in the Enemy Camp in 1966–1967*, Santa Monica, Calif.: RAND Corporation, 1969b. Government publication; not available to the general public.

————, *Terrorists—What Are They Like? How Some Terrorists Describe Their World and Actions*, Santa Monica, Calif.: RAND Corporation, N-1300-SL, 1979. Online at http://www.rand.org/pubs/notes/N1300/ (as of February 13, 2006).

Khong, Yuen Foong, *Analogies at War: Korea, Munich, Dien Bien Phu, and the Vietnam Decisions of 1965*, Princeton, N.J.: Princeton University Press, 1992.

Knickmeyer, Ellen, "Iraqi Premier Decries Torture of Detainees; Jafari Reacts to Discovery of Abuses," *The Washington Post*, December 13, 2005, p. A18.

Koch, J. A., *The Chieu Hoi Program in South Vietnam, 1963–1971*, Santa Monica, Calif.: RAND Corporation, R-1172-ARPA, 1973.

Komer, Robert W., *Organization and Management of the New Model Pacification Program—1966–1969*, Santa Monica, Calif.: RAND Corporation, D-20104-ARPA, 1970.

————, *Bureaucracy Does Its Thing: Institutional Constraints on U.S.-GVN Performance in Vietnam*, Santa Monica, Calif.: RAND Corporation, R-967-ARPA, 1972a. Online at http://www.rand.org/pubs/reports/R967/ (as of February 13, 2006).

————, *The Malayan Emergency in Retrospect: Organization of a Successful Counterinsurgency Effort*, Santa Monica, Calif.: RAND Corporation, R-957-ARPA, 1972b. Online at http://www.rand.org/pubs/reports/R957/ (as of February 13, 2006).

Komer, Robert, Steven L. Canby, Colin Frank Bell, E. W. Boyd, and A. A. Barbour, *Restructuring NATO Forces to Compensate for MBFR*, Santa Monica, Calif.: RAND Corporation, R-1231-ARPA/ISA/DDPAE, 1973. Not reviewed for public release.

Krepinevich, Andrew F., Jr., "How to Win in Iraq," *Foreign Affairs*, September/October 2005. Online at http://www.foreignaffairs.org/20050901faessay84508/andrew-f-krepinevich-jr/how-to-win-in-iraq.html (as of February 13, 2006).

Leites, Nathan Constantin, *The Operational Code of the Politburo*, New York.: McGraw-Hill, 1951.

Leites, Nathan Constantin, and Charles Wolf, Jr., *Rebellion and Authority: An Analytic Essay on Insurgent Conflicts*, Santa Monica, Calif.: RAND Corporation, R-0462-ARPA, 1970. Online at http://www.rand.org/pubs/reports/R0462/ (as of February 14, 2006).

Long, Austin, "Counterinsurgency in Vietnam," in Adam Stulberg and Michael Salomone, *Managing Defense Transformation: Agency, Culture, and Service Change*, Burlington, Vt.: Ashgate, forthcoming.

Lynn, John A., "Patterns of Insurgency and Counterinsurgency," *Military Review*, July/August 2005, pp. 22–27. Online at http://usacac.leavenworth.army.mil/CAC/milreview/download/English/JulAug05/lynn.pdf (as of February 13, 2006).

Mao Zedong, *On Guerrilla War*, New York: Praeger, 1961.

Maranto, Robert, and Paula S. Tuchman, "Knowing the Rational Peasant: The Creation of Rival Incentive Structures in Vietnam," *Journal of Peace Research*, Vol. 29, No. 3, 1992, pp. 249–264.

March, James G., and Chip Heath, *A Primer on Decision Making: How Decisions Happen*, New York: Free Press, 1994.

Marquis, Jefferson P., "The Other Warriors: American Social Science and Nation Building in Vietnam," *Diplomatic History*, Vol. 24, No. 1, 2000, pp. 79–106.

Marshall, S. L. A., *Men Against Fire: The Problem of Battle Command in Future War*, New York: William Morrow and Co., 1947.

Maullin, Richard L., *Soldiers, Guerrillas, and Politics in Colombia*, Santa Monica, Calif.: RAND Corporation, R-0630-ARPA, 1971. Online at http://www.rand.org/pubs/reports/R0630/ (as of February 16, 2006).

May, Andrew, *The RAND Corporation and the Dynamics of American Strategic Thought, 1946–1962*, Atlanta, Ga.: Emory University, Ph.D. thesis, 1999.

May, Ernest R., *"Lessons" of the Past: The Use and Misuse of History in American Foreign Policy*, New York: Oxford University Press, 1973.

McNerney, Michael J., "Stabilization and Reconstruction in Afghanistan: Are PRTs a Model or a Muddle?" *Parameters*, Vol. 35, No. 4, Winter 2005–2006, pp. 32–46. Online at http://carlisle-www.army.mil/usawc/Parameters/05winter/mcnerney.pdf (as of February 15, 2006).

Melnik, C., *Insurgency and Counterinsurgency in Algeria*, Santa Monica, Calif.: RAND Corporation, D-10671-1-ISA, 1964.

Merom, Gil, *How Democracies Lose Small Wars: State, Society, and the Failures of France in Algeria, Israel in Lebanon, and the United States in Vietnam*, Cambridge and New York: Cambridge University Press, 2003.

Meyer, Christina, Jennifer Duncan, and Bruce Hoffman, *Force-on-Force Attacks, Their Implications for the Defense of U.S. Nuclear Facilities*, Santa Monica, Calif.: RAND Corporation, N-3638-DOE, 1993. Online at http://www.rand.org/pubs/notes/N3638/ (as of February 13, 2006).

Mockaitis, Thomas R., *British Counterinsurgency 1919–60*, New York: St. Martin's Press, 1990.

———, *British Counterinsurgency in the Post-Imperial Era*, Manchester and New York: Manchester University Press, 1995.

Moyar, Mark, *Phoenix and the Birds of Prey: The CIA's Secret Campaign to Destroy the Viet Cong*, Annapolis, Md.: Naval Institute Press, 1997.

Mullainathan, Sendhil, and Richard Thaler, "Behavioral Economics," in Neil J. Smelser and Paul B. Baltes, eds., *International Encyclopedia of the Social and Behavioral Sciences*, Amsterdam: Elsevier, 2002, pp. 1094–1100.

National Security Council, *National Strategy for Victory in Iraq*, Washington, D.C.: National Security Council, November 2005. Online at http://www.whitehouse.gov/infocus/iraq/iraq_national_strategy_20051130.pdf (as of February 14, 2006).

Neustadt, Richard E., and Ernest R. May, *Thinking in Time: The Uses of History for Decision-Makers*, New York: Free Press, 1986.

NSC. See National Security Council.

Packer, George, *The Assassin's Gate: America in Iraq*, New York: Farrar, Straus, and Giroux, 2005.

Pakenham, Thomas, *The Boer War*, New York: Random House, 1979.

Pauker, Guy J., *Notes on Non-Military Measures in Control of Insurgency*, Santa Monica, Calif.: RAND Corporation, P-2642, 1962. Online at http://www.rand.org/pubs/papers/P2642 (as of July 6, 2006).

———, *Government Responses to Armed Insurgency in Southeast Asia: A Comparative Examination of Failures and Successes and Their Likely Implications for the Future*, Santa Monica, Calif.: RAND Corporation, P-7081, 1985. Online at http://www.rand.org/pubs/papers/P7081/ (as of February 14, 2006).

Paxson, Edwin W., *The Sierra Project—A Study of Limited Wars: Presented to the Air Staff in Washington*, Santa Monica, Calif.: RAND Corporation, B-41, 1958.

Petersen, Roger Dale, *Resistance and Rebellion: Lessons from Eastern Europe*, Cambridge and New York: Cambridge University Press, 2001.

Pike, Douglas Eugene, *Viet Cong: The Organization and Techniques of the National Liberation Front of South Vietnam*, Cambridge, Mass.: M.I.T. Press, 1966.

Pohle, Victoria, *The Viet Cong in Saigon: Tactics and Objectives During the Tet Offensive*, Santa Monica, Calif.: RAND Corporation, RM-5799-ISA/ARPA, 1969. Online at http://www.rand.org/pubs/research_memoranda/RM5799/ (as of February 15, 2006).

Popkin, Samuel L., "Pacification: Politics and the Village," *Asian Survey*, Vol. 10, No. 8, 1970, pp. 662–671.

―――, *The Rational Peasant: The Political Economy of Rural Society in Vietnam*, Berkeley, Calif.: University of California Press, 1979.

Posen, Barry R., "Inadvertent Nuclear War? Escalation and NATO's Northern Flank," *International Security*, Vol. 7, No. 2, Autumn 1982, pp. 28–54.

―――, "Command of the Commons: The Military Foundation of U.S. Hegemony," *International Security*, Vol. 28, No. 1, 2003, pp. 5–46.

Pye, Lucian W., *Lessons from the Malayan Struggle Against Communism*, Cambridge, Mass.: MIT Center for International Studies, 1958.

―――, *Observations on the Chieu Hoi Program*, Santa Monica, Calif.: RAND Corporation, RM-4864-1-ISA/ARPA, 1966.

Quinlivan, James T., "Force Requirements in Stability Operations," *Parameters*, Vol. 25, No. 4, 1995, pp. 59–69. Online at http://carlisle-www.army.mil/usawc/Parameters/1995/quinliv.htm (as of February 13, 2006).

Ramakrishna, Kumar, "'Bribing the Reds to Give Up': Rewards Policy in the Malayan Emergency," *War in History*, Vol. 9, No. 3, 2002, pp. 332–353.

Record, Jeffrey, *The Wrong War: Why We Lost in Vietnam*, Annapolis, Md.: Naval Institute Press, 1998.

Richey, Warren, "Iraq's Other Disarmament Challenge: Small Arms," *Christian Science Monitor*, May 2, 2003, p. 3.

Roberts, Steven, "Six Rand Experts Support Pullout," *The New York Times*, October 9, 1969a.

―――, "Four at Rand Ask Gradual Troop Cuts," *The New York Times*, October 18, 1969b.

Rosenau, William, *US Internal Security Assistance to South Vietnam: Insurgency, Subversion, and Public Order*, London and New York: Routledge, 2005.

Rostow, W. W., *Economic Growth: A Non-Communist Manifesto*, Cambridge, Mass.: MIT Center for International Studies, 1959.

Schilling, G. F., *Analytic Model of Border Control*, Santa Monica, Calif.: RAND Corporation, RM-6250-ARPA, 1970. Online at http://www.rand.org/pubs/research_memoranda/RM6250/ (as of February 15, 2006).

Schnaubelt, Christopher M., "After the Fight: Interagency Operations," *Parameters*, Vol. 35, No. 4, Winter 2005–2006, pp. 47–61. Online at http://carlisle-www.army.mil/usawc/Parameters/05winter/schnaube.pdf (as of February 15, 2006).

Schwarz, Benjamin, *American Counterinsurgency Doctrine and El Salvador: The Frustrations of Reform and the Illusions of Nation Building*, Santa Monica, Calif.: RAND Corporation, R-4042-USDP, 1991. Online at http://www.rand.org/pubs/reports/R4042/ (as of February 13, 2006).

Scott, James C., "Revolution in the Revolution: Peasants and Commissars," *Theory and Society*, Vol. 7, Nos. 1–2, 1979, pp. 97–134.

Selznick, Philip, *The Organizational Weapon: A Study of Bolshevik Strategy and Tactics*, Santa Monica, Calif.: RAND Corporation, R-201, 1952.

Sepp, Kalev I., "Best Practices in Counterinsurgency," *Military Review*, May/ June 2005. Online at http://www.findarticles.com/p/articles/mi_m0PBZ/ is_3_85/ai_n14695879 (as of February 14, 2006).

Serchuk, Vance, "Hearts and Minds: Innovative Teams Are Building Good-will at the Grass-Roots Level," *Armed Forces Journal*, November 2005. Online at http://www.armedforcesjournal.com/story.php?F=1169818_1105 (as of February 16, 2006).

Shafer, D. Michael, *Deadly Paradigms: The Failure of U.S. Counterinsurgency Policy*, Princeton, N.J.: Princeton University Press, 1988.

Sheehan, Neil, *A Bright, Shining Lie: John Paul Vann and America in Vietnam*, New York: Vintage, 1989.

Shils, Edward A., and Morris Janowitz, "Cohesion and Disintegration in the Wehrmacht in World War II," *The Public Opinion Quarterly*, Vol. 12, No. 2, 1948, pp. 280–315.

Shulimson, Jack, and Major Charles M. Johnson, U.S. Marine Corps, *U.S. Marines in Vietnam: The Landing and the Buildup*, Washington, D.C.: History and Museums Division, U.S. Marine Corps, 1965.

Simulmatics Corporation, *Improving Effectiveness of the Chieu Hoi Program: Revised Final Report*, Cambridge, Mass.: Simulmatics Corporation, 1967.

Sorensen, Theodore C., *Kennedy*, New York: Harper and Row, 1965.

Staniland, Paul, "Defeating Transnational Insurgencies: The Best Offense Is a Good Fence," *The Washington Quarterly*, Vol. 29, No. 1, Winter 2005–2006, pp. 21–40.

Starry, Donn A., *Mounted Combat in Vietnam*, Washington, D.C.: Department of the Army, 1979.

Sunderland, Riley, *Organizing Counterinsurgency in Malaya, 1947–1960*, Santa Monica, Calif.: RAND Corporation, RM-4171-ISA, 1964a. Online at http://www.rand.org/pubs/research_memoranda/RM4171/ (as of February 14, 2006).

———, *Resettlement and Food Control in Malaya*, Santa Monica, Calif.: RAND Corporation, RM-4173-ISA, 1964b. Online at http://www.rand.org/pubs/research_memoranda/RM4173/ (as of February 14, 2006).

———, *Winning the Hearts and Minds of the People: Malaya, 1948–1960*, Santa Monica, Calif.: RAND Corporation, RM-4174-ISA, 1964c. Online at http://www.rand.org/pubs/research_memoranda/RM4174/ (as of February 14, 2006).

Sweetland, A., *Item Analysis of the HES (Hamlet Evaluation System)*, Santa Monica, Calif.: RAND Corporation, D-17634-ARPA/AGILE, 1968.

Tang, Truong Nhu, David Chanoff, and Van Toai Doan, *A Viet Cong Memoir: An Inside Account of the Vietnam War and Its Aftermath*, San Diego: Harcourt Brace Jovanovich, 1985.

Taw, Jennifer, and Bruce Hoffman, *The Urbanization of Insurgency: The Potential Challenge to U.S. Army Operations*, Santa Monica, Calif.: RAND Corporation, MR-398-A, 1994. Online at http://www.rand.org/pubs/monograph_reports/MR398/ (as of February 13, 2006).

Taylor, Maxwell D., *The Uncertain Trumpet*, New York: Harper, 1960.

Tomlinson, Chris, "Reconstruction Team Launched in Babylon," *Associated Press Online*, November 21, 2005.

Trinquier, Roger, *Modern Warfare: A French View of Counterinsurgency*, New York: Praeger, 1964.

Twomey, Christopher P., "The McNamara Line and the Turning Point for Civilian Scientist-Advisers in Defence Policy, 1966–1968," *Minerva*, Vol. 37, No. 3, 1999, pp. 235–258.

U.S. Marine Corps, *Small Wars Manual: United States Marine Corps, 1940*, Manhattan, Kan.: Sunflower Univ. Press, 1972.

Weiner, Milton G., and Marvin Schaffer, *Border Security in South Vietnam*, Santa Monica, Calif.: RAND Corporation, R-0572-ARPA, 1971. Online at http://www.rand.org/pubs/reports/R0572/ (as of February 15, 2006).

Wells, Tom, *Wild Man: The Life and Times of Daniel Ellsberg*, New York: Palgrave, 2001.

West, Francis James, *The Enclave: Some U.S. Military Efforts in Ly Tin District, Quang Tin Province, 1966–1968*, Santa Monica, Calif.: RAND Corporation, RM-5941-ARPA, 1969a. Online at http://www.rand.org/pubs/research_memoranda/RM5941/ (as of February 15, 2006).

———, *The Strike Teams: Tactical Performance and Strategic Potential*, Santa Monica, Calif.: RAND Corporation, P-3987, 1969b. Online at http://www.rand.org/pubs/papers/P3987/ (as of February 15, 2006).

———, *The Village*, Madison, Wis.: University of Wisconsin Press, 1985.

Wohlstetter, Albert, *The Delicate Balance of Terror*, Santa Monica, Calif.: RAND Corporation, P-1472, 1958. Online at http://www.rand.org/publications/classics/wohlstetter/P1472/P1472.html (as of February 13, 2006).

———, *On Vietnam and Bureaucracy*, Santa Monica, Calif.: RAND Corporation, D-17276-1-ISA/ARPA, July 17, 1968a. Online at http://www.rand.org/publications/classics/wohlstetter/D17276.1/D17276.1.html (as of February 13, 2006).

———, *Comments on the Wolf-Leites Manuscript: "Rebellion and Authority,"* D(L)-17701-ARPA/AGILE, Santa Monica, Calif.: RAND Corporation, August 30, 1968b. Online at http://www.rand.org/publications/classics/wohlstetter/DL17701/DL17701.html (as of February 13, 2006).

Wolf, Charles, Jr., *Insurgency and Counterinsurgency: New Myths and Old Realities*, Santa Monica, Calif.: RAND Corporation, P-3132-1, 1965. Online at http://www.rand.org/pubs/papers/P3132-1/ (as of February 14, 2006).

Wolf, Charles, Marilee Lawrence, Aaron S. Gurwitz, E. D. Brunner, and K. C. Yeh, *The Costs of the Soviet Empire*, Santa Monica, Calif.: RAND Corporation, R-3073/1-NA, 1983. Online at http://www.rand.org/pubs/reports/R3073.1 (as of July 6, 2006).

Wong, Leonard, *Why They Fight: Combat Motivation in the Iraq War*, Carlisle, Pa.: Strategic Studies Institute and U.S. Army War College, 2003. Online at http://permanent.access.gpo.gov/lps35591/whyfight.pdf (as of February 16, 2006).

Zwick, C. J., Charles A. Cooper, Hans Heymann, and Richard H. Moorsteen, *U.S. Economic Assistance in Vietnam: A Proposed Reorientation*, Santa Monica, Calif.: RAND Corporation, R-0430-AID, 1964.